IN YOUR OWN WORDS

IN YOUR OWN WORDS

A Beginner's Guide to Writing

REVISED EDITION

BY SYLVIA CASSEDY

Thomas Y. Crowell   New York

Library of Congress Cataloging-in-Publication Data
Cassedy, Sylvia.
   In your own words : a beginner's guide to writing / by Sylvia Cassedy.—
Rev. ed.
      p.   cm.
   Includes bibliographical references.
   Summary: A guide to writing prose, both fiction and nonfiction, and poetry.
   ISBN 0-690-04821-1.—ISBN 0-690-04823-8 (lib. bdg.)
   1. English language—Composition and exercises—Juvenile literature.
[1. English language—Composition and exercises.   2. Creative writing.]
I. Title.
LB1576.C318   1990   89-78079
808′.042—dc20   CIP
                                                                        AC

10 9 8 7 6 5 4 3 2 1
REVISED EDITION

Every effort has been made to trace the ownership of all copyrighted material and to secure the necessary permission to reprint these selections. The author and publisher regret any inadvertent errors in the use of any material and will be happy to make the necessary correction in future printings. Thanks are due to the following for permission to reprint the materials listed:

   Richard Aldridge for "The Pine Bough" from *An Apology Both Ways*. Reprinted by permission of the author.
   Peggy Bennett for "Plain Talk for a Pachyderm." Reprinted by permission of the author.
   Curtis Brown, Ltd., for "The Sound of Night" from *Halfway* by Maxine Kumin. Copyright © 1961 by Maxine W. Kumin. Reprinted by permission of Curtis Brown, Ltd.

Adam Carlson for "Cardinal on the snow." Reprinted by permission of the author.

Amy Cassedy for "The clicking cricket." Reprinted by permission of the author.

Edward S. Cassedy for "Red dragonfly" by Soseki and "A discovery" by Yayu, both translated by Sylvia Cassedy and Kunihiro Suetake, from *Birds, Frogs, and Moonlight.* Copyright © 1967 by Doubleday & Company, Inc. Reprinted by permission of Edward S. Cassedy.

Doubleday & Company, Inc., for the excerpt from "Song of the Pop-bottlers" from *A Bowl of Bishop* by Morris Bishop. Copyright 1954 by Morris Bishop; "Up the barley rows" from *Introduction to Haiku* translated by Harold G. Henderson. Copyright © 1958 by Harold G. Henderson; "The Waking" from *The Collected Poems of Theodore Roethke* by Theodore Roethke. Copyright 1948 by Theodore Roethke. All selections reprinted by permission of Doubleday & Company, Inc., a division of Bantam, Doubleday, Dell Publishing Group, Inc.

The Estate of Norma Millay Ellis for "Counting-out Rhyme" by Edna St. Vincent Millay. From *Collected Poems,* Harper & Row, Publishers, Inc. Copyright 1928, 1955 by Edna St. Vincent Millay and Norma Millay Ellis. Reprinted by permission.

Dave Etter for "Snow Country" from *Go Read the River* published by University of Nebraska Press. Reprinted by permission of the author.

Harcourt Brace Jovanovich, Inc., for "Old Deep Sing-song" from *Wind Song* by Carl Sandburg. Copyright © 1958 by Carl Sandburg, renewed 1986 by Margaret Sandburg, Janet Sandburg and Helga Sandburg Crile; excerpt from "Swimmers" from *Long Feud* by Louis Untermeyer. Copyright © 1962 by Louis Untermeyer. Both selections reprinted by permission of Harcourt Brace Jovanovich, Inc.

Harper & Row, Publishers, Inc., for "Elevator" and "Greenhouse" from *Roomrimes* by Sylvia Cassedy. Copyright © 1987 by Sylvia Cassedy; excerpt from "The Ruined City" by Pao Chao, translated by Jerome Ch'en and Michael Bullock in *Poems of Solitude* by Jerome Ch'en and Michael Bullock. Copyright © 1960 by Jerome Ch'en and Michael Bullock; "Cat!" from *Eleanor Farjeon's Poems for Children* by Eleanor Farjeon, published by J. B. Lippincott. Originally published in *Sing for Your Supper* by Eleanor Farjeon. Copyright 1938, renewed 1966 by Eleanor Farjeon; "Spring" from *Dogs and Dragons, Trees and Dreams* by Karla Kuskin. Copyright © 1958 by Karla Kuskin. All selections reprinted by permission of Harper & Row, Publishers, Inc.

Janet Hart and Marshall Head for "Thaw" by Eunice Tietjens. Copyright 1934, © 1962 by Rand McNally & Company. First appeared in *Child Life Magazine*. Reprinted by permission of Janet Hart and Marshall Head.

David Henderson for "Number 5—December" from *Felix of the Silent Forest* published by Poets Press. Copyright © 1966 by David Henderson. Reprinted by permission of the author.

Henry Holt and Company, Inc., for "One Guess" by Robert Frost from *The Poetry of Robert Frost* edited by Edward Connery Lathem. Copyright © 1969 by Holt, Rinehart and Winston, Inc. Copyright © 1962 by Robert Frost. Copyright © 1975 by Lesley Frost Ballantine. Reprinted by permission of Henry Holt and Company, Inc.

Stephen Janosco for "The Garden Hose" by Beatrice Janosco. Reprinted by permission of the author.

David Kherdian for "Above the Moving River" from *Homage to Adana* by David Kherdian, published by Giligia Press. Copyright © 1970, 1971 by David Kherdian. Reprinted by permission of the author.

Alfred A. Knopf, Inc., for "Mirror" from *The Carpentered Hen and Other Tame Creatures* by John Updike. Copyright © 1957 by John Updike; excerpt from "The Great Scarf of Birds" and "Winter Ocean" from *Telephone Poles and Other Poems* by John Updike. Copyright © 1960 by John Updike; excerpt from "Velvet Shoes" by Elinor Wylie from *The Collected Poems of Elinor Wylie.* Copyright 1921 by Alfred A. Knopf, Inc., renewed 1949 by William Rose Benet. All selections reprinted by permission of Alfred A. Knopf, Inc.

Rozanne Knudson for "Living Tenderly" by May Swenson. Copyright © 1963 by May Swenson. Reprinted by permission of Rozanne Knudson.

Alice Lattimore for the first stanza of "Dolphin Seen Alone" from *Poems of Three Decades* by Richmond Lattimore, published by Charles Scribner's Sons. Reprinted by permission of Alice Lattimore.

Anna Law for "Anger." Reprinted by permission of the author.

Liveright Publishing Corporation for "r-p-o-p-h-e-s-s-a-g-r" reprinted from *No Thanks* by E. E. Cummings, edited by George James

Firmage, by permission of Liveright Publishing Corporation. Copyright 1935 by E. E. Cummings. Copyright © 1968 by Marion Morehouse Cummings. Copyright © 1973, 1978 by the Trustees for the E. E. Cummings Trust. Copyright © 1973, 1978 by George James Firmage.

Pierre A. MacKay for "I Wish My Tongue Were a Quiver" by L. A. MacKay. Reprinted by permission of Pierre A. MacKay.

Lillian Morrison for "The Sidewalk Racer" from *The Sidewalk Racer and Other Poems of Sports and Motion.* Copyright © 1977 by Lillian Morrison. Reprinted by permission of the author.

William Morrow and Company, Inc., for "Winter Poem" from *My House* by Nikki Giovanni. Copyright © 1972 by Nikki Giovanni. Reprinted by permission of William Morrow and Company, Inc.

New Directions Publishing Corporation for "In a Station of the Metro" from *Personae* by Ezra Pound. Copyright 1926 by Ezra Pound; "Poem," "This Is Just to Say," and "The Red Wheelbarrow" from *Collected Poems: Volume I: 1901–1939* by William Carlos Williams. Copyright 1938 by New Directions Publishing Corporation. All selections reprinted by permission of New Directions Publishing Corporation.

The New Statesman for "A Warm Winter Day" by Julian Cooper from *The New Statesman,* 17 January 1964. Reprinted by permission of *The New Statesman.*

Raymond R. Patterson for "Black All Day" and "Glory, Glory" from *26 Ways of Looking at a Black Man* published by Grosset & Dunlap. Copyright © 1969 by Raymond R. Patterson. Reprinted by permission of the author.

Penguin Books Ltd. for "Against the broad sky" by Takahama Kyoshi from *The Penguin Book of Japanese Verse* translated by Geoffrey Bownas and Anthony Thwaite. Copyright © 1964 Geoffrey Bownas and Anthony Thwaite. Reprinted by permission of Penguin Books Ltd.

Peter Pauper Press, Inc., for "Bird droppings" and "Morning-misted street" by Buson; "The night is hot" by Issa; "Good morning, sparrow" and "See the red berries" by Shiki; "The heavy wagon" by Shoha; "As I pick it up" by Taigi; "The floating heron" by Zuiryu; all selections from *The Four Seasons.* All selections reprinted by permission of Peter Pauper Press, Inc.

Peters, Fraser & Dunlop Ltd. for "On a Sundial" from *Sonnets and*

Verse by Hilaire Belloc. Reprinted by permission of the Peters Fraser & Dunlop Group Ltd.

G. P. Putnam's Sons for "Snow" from *Everything and Anything* by Dorothy Aldis. Copyright 1925–1927, renewed 1953–1955 by Dorothy Aldis. Reprinted by permission of G. P. Putnam's Sons.

Random House, Inc., for "Interlude III" from *Selected Poems* by Karl Shapiro. Copyright 1944, renewed 1962 by Karl Shapiro. Reprinted by permission of Random House, Inc.

Richard Rieu for one stanza of "Portrait of a House" from *The Flattered Flying Fish and Other Poems* by E. V. Rieu, published by E. P. Dutton & Company, Inc., and A. B. P. International. Reprinted by permission of Richard Rieu.

Louise H. Sclove for "Motto for a Dog House" from *Lyric Laughter* by Arthur Guiterman. Copyright 1915, 1918, 1923 by Arthur Guiterman. Copyright 1929, 1939 by E. P. Dutton & Co., Inc. Reprinted by permission of Louise H. Sclove.

Gail M. Shearer for excerpt from "Fireflies" from *Skipping Along Alone* by Winifred Welles, published by Macmillan Company. Reprinted by permission of Gail M. Shearer, Livermore, California.

William Jay Smith for excerpt from "The Toaster" from *Laughing Time: Nonsense Poems* by William Jay Smith, published by Delacorte Press, 1980, copyright © 1955, 1957, 1980 by William Jay Smith. Reprinted by permission of William Jay Smith.

Lloyd Sarett Stockdale for "The Loon," a poem by Lew Sarett, from *Many, Many Moons,* copyright 1920 and 1948 by Lew Sarett. Reprinted by permission of Lloyd Sarett Stockdale.

Viking Penguin Inc., for excerpt from "Kangaroo" from *The Complete Poems of D. H. Lawrence,* edited by Vivian de Sola Pinto and F. Warren Roberts. Copyright © 1964, 1971 by Angelo Ravagli and C. M. Weekley, executors of the Estate of Frieda Lawrence Ravagli. All rights reserved. Reprinted by permission of Viking Penguin Inc.

Robert Wallace for "The Garden Snail." Copyright © 1956 by Robert Wallace. Reprinted by permission of the author.

World Book, Inc., for excerpt from "Frogs" from *The World Book Encyclopedia.* Copyright © 1988 by World Book, Inc. Reprinted by permission of World Book, Inc.

Adam Yarmolinsky for "Ballet School" by Babette Deutsch from *The Collected Poems of Babette Deutsch* published by Doubleday & Company, Inc. Copyright © 1969 by Babette Deutsch. Reprinted by permission of Adam Yarmolinsky.

Brett Yoches for "Razor Clam Shell." Reprinted by permission of the author.

Laura (Shtrick) Yoskowitz for "Face to face" by Laura Shtrick. Reprinted by permission of Laura (Shtrick) Yoskowitz.

Alison Young for "A Windy Day" from *Collected Poems* by Andrew Young, edited by Leonard Clark. Reprinted by permission of Alison Young.

Hilda Conkling's "Red Rooster" is reprinted from *Poems by a Little Girl* published by Frederick A. Stokes Company, 1920. Copyright 1949 by Hilda Conkling.

Emily Dickinson's "A bird came down the walk" and "I like to see it lap the miles" are reprinted from *The Complete Works of Emily Dickinson* edited by Thomas H. Johnson, published by Little, Brown and Company.

Strickland Gillilan's "Lines on the Antiquity of Microbes" is reprinted from *A Third Treasury of the Familiar,* edited by Ralph L. Woods, published by Macmillan Publishing Co., 1970.

Thomas Hardy's "Birds at Winter Nightfall" is reprinted from *The Complete Poems of Thomas Hardy* edited by James Gibson, published by Macmillan Publishing Co., 1978.

Alicia Loy Johnson's "A Black-Poetry Day" is reprinted from *Nine Black Poets* published by Moore Publishing Company.

Newman Levy's "Midsummer Jingle" is reprinted from *Gay But Wistful* published by Alfred A. Knopf, Inc.

The excerpt from Humbert Wolfe's "The Grey Squirrel" is reprinted from *Kensington Gardens* published by Doubleday & Company.

The excerpt from William Butler Yeats's "The Lake Isle of Innisfree" is reprinted from *The Poems of W. B. Yeats: A New Edition,* edited by Richard J. Finneran, published by Macmillan Publishing Co., 1983.

The author is grateful to Yuzo and Kazuko Honda for providing background information for the haiku chapter.

*To all the young students whose poems and stories
have been the inspiration of this book,
and especially to Amy and Susannah,
students and daughters alike.*

Contents

POETRY

Author's Note

Everybody has something to write about.

At every moment in your life there is an event taking place that is important enough to be put down in words.

An event can be a big and noisy thing, like a football game or a parade. Or it can be small and quiet, like the tickle on your finger when you stroke a beetle's back or the flutter in your nostrils when you pass a hot-dog stand.

An event can take place inside you, where no one else can see. A daydream is an event, and so is a secret wish. A burst of joy or anger is an event, and so is a rush of whispered words that bounce around your head. A new-found fact is an event. So is a stopping still to wonder at a bulldozer or the moon.

Anything that you are aware of is an event in your life. It is yours alone. Private as a daydream or public as a parade, it happens only to you. No one else senses it just as you do. That is why when you write about it, you reveal something new to the whole world.

Taking notice of the events in your life and turning them into words of your very own is what creative writing is all about.

This book will help you learn how.

HOW TO
BEGIN

1
Taking Notice

The sixteenth-century sculptor Michelangelo used to imagine that every block of stone he set out to carve contained a fully formed statue waiting to be released. All he had to do was chip away everything that wasn't statue, and there it would be—a horse, an angel, a beautiful woman, or a tiny cherub.

Ideas for stories and poems are like imprisoned statues. They lie hidden in everything you can see or hear or put your hand on—every flower, every flake of snow, every shell; every shoelace, every potato chip, every wad of gum. They too are waiting to be released, not with a hammer and a chisel, but with a notebook and a pen.

Ideas are all around you, sometimes no farther than the reach of your hand. They are inside you as well, sometimes no louder than a whisper. The trouble is, you may not know they are there. Discovering them is like searching for materials for a collage. When you need bits and scraps of things to glue onto your art construction, you suddenly find quantities of old buttons and ribbons, onion bags and tissue-paper wads, steel wool and peanut shells, lying on sidewalks and supermarket floors, in kitchen drawers and trash cans. They were always there, but you had never seen them before because you hadn't needed them. Ideas for stories and poems are always there too. You have to need them to find them.

Ideas are small to begin with, and they come little by little. The story or poem that makes you ask, "How did anyone think all that up?" did not spring forth with its complicated adventures or perfect rhymes all worked out from beginning to end. It started as a tiny thought, no bigger perhaps than a single word. And it grew; not all at once, but in bits and pieces: an idea here, a phrase there.

Each bit, each piece, each idea, each phrase, started out with something noticed. To find the idea imprisoned in the snowflake, you must pay attention to the snowflake itself. Writing begins by taking notice. Taking notice of a spider scaling a web, taking notice of a football smacking the ground. Taking notice of a word that tingles your ear, taking notice of a subway's whine on the tracks. Taking notice of things, too, that you cannot see or hear, but only feel. Taking notice of the way you want to cry when you hear a special song, taking notice of the way your heart stops when you come upon a sparrow lying dead against the curb.

How do you learn to take notice? Easy. Pick something up and look at it. Anything will do, but if it's been around a long time and shows lots of signs of wear and tear, it will have more details to take notice of. A plastic bottle of glue would be fine. So would a ruler, a shoelace, a pencil, a wristwatch, or a Monopoly board. Each of these articles will bear markings that make it the only one of its kind in the world. See if you can find them.

The glue bottle may have a hardened white film, the kind that's fun to pick off with your fingernail, around the top. The ruler may have a flaky coating of crayon wax along the edge and a tracing of ink on each number. The shoelace may have a puff of threads where the plastic tip once was. The pencil may have a row of tooth marks along its side, the watch strap may have a crease around the hole that's used the most, and the Monopoly board may have a grease spot on Marvin Gardens.

Now, in a notebook—and it's important to keep all your writing in one notebook, so if you don't have one, get one—describe the object you have examined, mentioning especially those details that show it has been touched by a human creature. (Or a nonhuman one, for that matter; you may have decided to describe a dog's rubber bone.) Just tell what you see, like this:

A film of hardened glue surrounds the orange cap and covers the shoulders of the plastic bottle. A sprinkling of glitter—red, blue, and green—clings to the sides, and three tiny specks, all green, stick to the ear of the smirking bull on the label. All the big white letters across the front are carefully colored in with blue Magic Marker, and a broken pencil point is jammed in the nozzle. Sticking to the bottom, its edges curled and gray, is a red price label: 59¢.

You may leave it at that. You have taken notice of an object that a moment ago was insignificant, and you have

turned it into something special. Writing does that. The
words themselves, once they are down on paper and not
merely floating about in your ears, will also become special. Writing does that, too. Someday, now that the glue
bottle, or the ruler, or the shoelace, or the pencil, or the
wristwatch, or the Monopoly board, has taken on new
meaning, you may even want to write a poem about it.
There is some beautiful poetry written about some quite
ordinary things—plums, toes, oxtails, walnuts, beach
glass. There's even a poem about a toaster.

Or you may want to write some more right now. Give
your glue bottle an owner, if you like. You can call
her Josephine. Let Josephine do whatever she pleases
with the bottle of glue, but remember to describe it with
some of the details you have already observed. Like
this:

Josephine carefully picked off the film of glue around the
cap and scattered it on the table. A smudge of glitter rubbed
off on her thumb as she tried to pull out the pencil point
caught in the nozzle. She wondered if this was really the right
kind of glue to repair a shattered chandelier.

That might lead to more ideas. Maybe you will wonder about how the chandelier got smashed in the first
place. What had Josephine been doing? With whom?
Was she in her own house? In her grandmother's dining room? In Buckingham Palace? One by one, or all in
a jumble, ideas may come to you until, just maybe, you
will find that you have written a whole story, with a be-

ginning, a middle, and an end. And all from a bottle of glue.

Taking notice serves another purpose too: readers like to picture in their minds what is written in their books. If you take the trouble to observe the things you write about, you will make it easier for your reader to see what you have in mind. Instead of saying in a story that Bob "had a messy desk," tell what the desk looked like. Mention the chain of paper clips swinging from the drawer and the hills of pencil shavings on the blotter. Mention the looseleaf papers spilling over the sides and the dirty socks stuffed into the drinking glass. Describe a worn-out sneaker this way, too, or a shabby coat, an old football, or a cluttered kitchen table.

Once you have learned how to examine little things for little details, you can begin examining big things for big details. Imagine now that you are a detective entering your living room for the first time. You are there in search of evidence that someone has been in the room using things, handling them, touching them, wearing them out, messing them up. Look at the floor, the furniture, the television set. Look on shelves and tables and under the piano. Look in the wastebasket. Look for scratches and smudges and coffee-cup rings. Look for scuffs and skid marks and for jacks under the radiator. Don't forget that creatures other than humans leave their marks, too, so look for spiderwebs and cat hairs. Now, in your notebook, describe the room as you have

just observed it, scratches, dust balls, and all. Here's
how:

A vacuum cleaner had left long streaks across the rug—
mostly on the thick, plushy places under the tables, but also
on the thin spots in front of the sofa and chairs. An oily halo
surrounded each dial on the television set, and on its top lay
a scattering of fresh eraser crumbs. The keys on the piano
were smudged with gray. Candy wrappers lay curled in the
ashtrays, rusty paint peeled under the flowerpots on the radiator cover, and a picture hung crookedly on the wall. On the
mantel stood two candles, each with a single trickle of hardened wax along its side. Over one lampshade a spiderweb
puffed out like a silk balloon.

Leave aside your own living room for now, and make
one up out of your head. Close your eyes and imagine
four bare walls and a floor. Piece by piece, begin to add
furnishings. As you install each one, describe it in your
notebook as you described your own furniture with its
dents and scuffs and scatterings of crumbs. If your make-
believe room becomes agreeable enough, you might
want to invite one or two make-believe people into it and
let them move about among the worn sofa cushions and
the scarred piano bench.

That might be enough for a beginning. Leave your
notebook now and go off and walk the dog. Your mind
has a way of working even when you are not at your desk,
and hours or even days later you will cast your eye on
some new detail, and a new sentence that is just right for
your story will flash through your head. When you are

writing something that is important to you, it will follow you about wherever you go, picking up a stray thought here, a fragment of a phrase there, until you have a completed work that will cause your readers, too, to wonder, "How did anyone think all that up?"

Very often you fail to see things, even if they are right in front of your face, because you are too busy hearing them or feeling them. You feel the rain when you are caught in it, more than you see it, and you hear, rather than see, a singer. As a writer, though, you will want to know how such things look as well as how they feel or sound. Just for practice, try this: turn the sound of your television off and watch the screen: watch an orchestra, watch a crowd cheering a ball game, watch a baby. How can you tell, without hearing, that the baby is crying and not laughing? What does he do with his fists, his feet, his mouth, his eyes? How can you tell that someone is whispering a secret or screaming or giggling?

Play a game with a friend. Each of you write a description of somebody in the act of yawning or hiccuping or losing his temper. Tell only what he does with his body— how his head and shoulders move, what happens to his face, what he does with his hands. Remember—no sounds. Exchange descriptions and see if you can guess what the other's was about. Like this:

Eddie suddenly opened his mouth, gulped some air, tightened his eyes, crinkled his nose, hunched his shoulders, and covered his face. The next moment he violently expelled some air, closed his mouth, opened his eyes, straightened his nose, and lowered his shoulders. What did he just do?

Sneezed is what, and a second later he reached for a Kleenex.

You can describe objects as well as people in this manner, or whole landscapes, concentrating only on what you see. Imagine yourself on a windy day behind a tightly closed window overlooking a city street, a parking lot, a country field, or your own block. What are all the things you would *see* that would tell you a strong wind was blowing? What would be flying about? What would be scurrying along the ground, floating in the air, circling in the sky? How would people be walking? What happens to trees and grass and hair and scarves and squirrels' tails in a fierce wind? Write down everything you can think of. Don't make a list. Write out a whole sentence for each idea.

Andrew Young, a Scottish poet born in the late nineteenth century, might have been standing behind a closed window when he wrote the following poem about a countryside springing to life on a windy day. In it, the reader *sees* the wind but hears nothing:

A Windy Day

> The wind brings all dead things to life,
> Branches that lash the air like whips
> And dead leaves rolling in a hurry
> Or peering in a rabbit's bury

Or trying to push down a tree;
Gates that fly open to the wind
And close again behind,
And fields that are a flowing sea
And make the cattle look like ships;
Straws glistening and stiff
Lying on air as on a shelf
And pond that leaps to leave itself;
And feathers too that rise and float,
Each feather changed into a bird,
And line-hung sheets that crack and strain;
Even the sun-greened coat,
That through so many winds has served,
The scarecrow struggles to put on again.

ANDREW YOUNG

Andrew Young used his eyes like a movie camera,
moving them slowly across the panorama and stopping
now and then to zoom in on something special—a gate,
a flying straw, a pond, a floating feather, a line of wash,
a scarecrow struggling into its coat. As a writer, you will
use your eyes as a camera, too, sometimes to take stills
of glue bottles and butterfly wings, sometimes to sweep
across meadows and ball fields. Like Michelangelo's raw
blocks of stone, everything your camera sees, *everything*,
contains a work of art waiting to be let out.

2

Hearing, Smelling, Tasting, Touching

When you perceive the world around you, you do so not only with your eyes, but with your ears and nose and tongue and fingers as well. There are many things you know at once without using your eyes at all. When you answer the phone, for instance, and your uncle says, "Hello," you know who it is just by the sound of his voice: your ears tell you. When you're sitting in your room and your mother calls you to dinner, you know even before you reach the kitchen door that there's going to be fried chicken that night, because your nose tells you. There are things you can identify without seeing them or hearing them or even smelling them. The salt in a gulp of ocean water is one, and the spice in your pizza is another. You know they're there because your tongue tells you. Can you think of something you recognize immediately, even though you can't see it, hear it, smell it, or taste it? How about the wind? Or a stomachache? Feeling or touching, too, is a way of knowing that things are there.

Seeing, hearing, smelling, tasting, and touching.

These are the ways through which you discover your world. They are your five senses. Good writers use all of them to know their surroundings and to tell other people about them.

HEARING

Sounds drift into your ears all day long, sometimes dozens at a time. Refrigerators hum, dogs bark, car horns blow, stomachs rumble. Close your eyes for a moment, wherever you are, and listen. What do you hear now, soft things and loud, that you didn't notice when your eyes were open? Usually you ignore these sounds, and maybe it is just as well; if you paid close attention to the hum of a refrigerator all day long, you wouldn't get much of anything else done. But sounds tell you about your world just as sights do, sometimes more clearly, and writers must listen as well as look. To write of a snowy morning, you must know its sounds as well as its sights— the scrape of a shovel, the whine of a tire, the thwack of a snowball, the crunch of a boot—and to write of the night, you must listen to its whispers and its sighs.

Think once more of a windy scene, the one you watched from a sealed-up room. Open the window now and let all the wind sounds in. Close your eyes. What can you hear? The sounds of the wind itself, its howl at the chimney, its whistle through the cracks? What about the sounds of the things it disturbs—the bang of the shutters, the scrape of the leaves, the crack of the branches, the clatter of the garbage can rolling down the road?

In order to produce a sound, an object must move, however slightly. Stand outside for a while and watch things in motion—a rubber ball hitting a curb, a pigeon's beak scraping the sidewalk, a cat climbing a tree. Each movement has a sound of its own, and each sound can be described in words. There are hundreds of words in the English language that describe sounds: *boom* and *bang* and *roar*, of course, but also *snuffle* and *squish* and *chug* and *gurgle* and *caterwaul.*

Imagine that you have been led, blindfolded, to a mystery location. How would your ears tell you where you were? Suppose you were taken into a subway train. How would you know? The train itself makes noise, of course—the screech of its wheels rounding a curve and the hiss of its brakes. But what do you hear when the train stops? What are the sounds of passengers elbowing and sighing and reading newspapers and chewing gum? Now suppose you were taken to a beach. What sounds would tell you where you were? The ocean probably makes the loudest sound, but what might make the softest? A snail stirring inside its shell? A sea-gull feather falling on a rock? A drop of water rolling down a bathing suit? Big things often produce loud sounds and small things quiet ones, but not always. A giant cloud colliding with a mountain makes no sound at all, while the croak of a frog can be heard across a lake.

With your blindfold still on, make yourself very tiny. Crawl inside a rabbit burrow and listen. What can you hear? The scratching of paws, the sniffling of noses, and the scrape of a whisker against the earth? What else? Next visit a cell in a honeycomb, the inside of a bongo drum, the works of a cuckoo clock. What do you hear?

There are sounds that you hear in the summer and at no other time. What are they? How about autumn? Morning has its special sounds, too, and so has night. The following selection is filled with the scary night noise of a room after the lights have been turned off:

At night, when all the world is fast asleep, my room is wide awake. The light goes off, and suddenly the walls and doors begin to shake their creaking bones—a neck bone crackles here, an ankle rattles there, a thighbone snaps, a wristbone cracks, a rib cage buckles, shatters, breaks, and sends its splinters to the floor. The curtains at the window start to dance; the flounces on their dresses swish and rustle with each step, and somewhere from behind the closet door a shirt and robe take up the beat—rustle-swish, rustle-swish, rustle-swish.

Inside the walls whole families of—what? I cannot say— wake up and start their day. A dozen brooms the size of whisker tufts begin to sweep against the floor, and nails no longer than a mouse's claws are hammered one by one upon the wall.

The flies wake up. The swarms of flies that doze all day in curtain folds and balls of dust spring forth like pellets from a gun to fill the air with buzz and bang their heads against the window glass.

Outside, around the window frame, a crowd of whispers struggles to come in—the whisper of a bus, the whisper of a tree, the whisper of a pair of feet, the whisper of the rain, the whisper of a secret club of cats that meets outside the gate—all push and shove and slide upon the windowsill, and slip between the cracks at last, and rush about the room like flying birds.

Throughout the night the noise goes on, until at last the darkness fades, and all at once the brooms, the nails, the rustling skirts are put away, and I myself wake up to face the silence of the day.

SMELLING

Places and seasons have special smells too. Think of all the smells at the beach—suntan lotion, hot dogs, rotting fish, mustard, cigarette smoke, sneakers, talcum powder, wet bathing suits, the sea itself. You would know you were there even if you were blindfolded and your ears were stuffed, just as you would know you were in a doctor's office or the library or the subway or your grandma's house. Or your piano teacher's house, for that matter, or your best friend's. Everybody's house has its own wonderful mixture of cooking smells and cleaning smells and unidentifiable living smells that set it apart from everybody else's house.

There are lots of smells in your classroom, too— smells of marking pens and chalk dust, tuna sandwiches and wet boots—that help make it the special place it is. Try to find out what they are. Sniff around a bit, and see if you can come up with a list of ten items whose smells are special to your classroom.

Smells can not only tell you where you are—they can tell you where you have been. A single whiff of suntan lotion today can recall entire scenes of summers past, of packing for vacations and getting out bathing suits; and a sniff of autumn leaves can bring back the first day of school with its new shoes and stiff clothes. Try it. Poke your nose into a coffee can, a bag of oranges, a bar of soap, an ashtray, a wet glove. Do any of these smells remind you of something long ago? Cigars might smell of uncles or railway stations, and if so, you might write about them in just that way: "The cigar in the ashtray smelled like a large, drafty railroad station," or "The cigar smelled like Uncle Howard."

Some objects that surround you all the time have little quiet smells that you hardly know about. Find out what some of them are. Walk around your living room sometime when you don't have a cold, and press your nose against a sofa cushion, a wooden table, the back of the television, a lampshade, a shiny magazine, a telephone book, the soil in a flowerpot. Sometimes you discover these smells by accident, when you are crying into a pillow, for instance, or resting your head on your homework notebook.

Unfortunately, there aren't as many "smell" words as there are "sound" words in our language, and you may find that words like *sweet* or *musty* or *rotten* or *yucky* don't fill all your needs. They don't have to. Most of the time it is enough just to identify smells, or even to list them, in order to create the atmosphere you want. "The living room smelled of furniture polish, apples, and camphor" tells a lot about the living room and makes the reader feel that he is standing in it. In the following paragraph a cellar reveals itself by smell alone:

Everything in Hannah's grandfather's cellar smelled cold and damp and rotten. At first the smells came upon her one at a time as she picked her way down the stairs, and then they were all there together as she stood in the pale square of light near the potato bin. First came the smell of the walls—wet, ice-cold, and gray with mold. Then there was the smell of the newspapers, piled ceiling high in the corner and heavy with damp. Then the hill of sand beside the furnace, used throughout the day and night by Grandfather's three cats. Finally came the smell of rot—rotting apples, rotting potatoes, rotting onions, rotting wood, rotting harnesses, rotting shoes.

Cold and damp and rotten. It smelled wonderful, and Hannah loved it.

TASTING

If you use your nose when you write, your readers will use theirs when they read, and that is just what you want. You can also get them to use their taste buds. In the following poem, a delicious one, the poet offers us a bite of the cold, sweet plums that he sneaked from the refrigerator, and our mouths water along with his:

This Is Just to Say

I have eaten
the plums
that were in
the icebox

and which
you were probably
saving
for breakfast

> Forgive me
> they were delicious
> so sweet
> and so cold

WILLIAM CARLOS WILLIAMS

You, too, can share a delicious—or not so delicious—taste with your readers. Think of a food you absolutely love or absolutely hate. Write about its taste and write, too, about how it feels in your mouth—how the insides of your cheeks prickle and spurt when you take your first mouthful. Write about how you crush it with your molars if it's bubble gum, or how it squeezes between your teeth if it's mashed potatoes. Write about how part of it sticks to your gums and part of it cools if it's peanut butter and jelly, or how all of it turns your tongue to wool if it's spinach. Write about the tiny bubbles that burst in your throat and nose if it's root beer, or the rubbery bits that fasten themselves to your teeth if it's dates. Don't worry about a beginning sentence. Just start in, like this: "A sourball fuzzes the inside of my cheek, where I keep it while it's still big, so it won't slide down my throat. Every now and then I rub off some of its warm, sticky juice with my tongue."

Often the *feeling* of what you pop into your mouth is more enjoyable than the flavor, especially if it isn't meant to be eaten in the first place. It feels good to sink your teeth into the side of a pencil, even though painted wood is not very tasty, and to suck on a necklace of glass beads, or to soften a fingernail between your teeth, to chew on a torn balloon, to draw a hank of hair between your lips.

Some things get into your mouth by mistake—tears trickling into the corners of your lips, falling snowflakes stinging your tongue, ocean water rushing down your throat when you're tumbled by a wave—and they, too, have tastes that you notice and remember when you write.

TOUCHING

Finally, to know the world you write about, you must touch it. Touch and feel. Wander around your classroom or your house and find half a dozen things that might be fun to touch. Some, like cats' ears and velvet ribbons, will feel good. Others, like sandpaper and cacti, will not. Try them anyway. Notice the different ways you go about feeling different objects: you squeeze balloons, dig your fingernails into Styrofoam balls, pop plastic bubbles, roll clay between your palms. You rub satin against your cheek, run your thumb along a pebble, crush a wad of cotton, let sand run through your fingers. And you needn't always use your hands; you feel snow and windowpanes with your nose, and frost with the tips of your ears. Here's a poem about feeling with feet:

Thaw

The snow is soft
   and how it squashes!
"Galumph, galumph!"
   go my galoshes.

EUNICE TIETJENS

When slush mushes under your galoshes or a ladybug tickles the tip of your finger, you feel in only one spot at a time, but when you stand in the wind or take a bath, you feel all over, from head to toe. Here is part of a poem about an all-over-the-body feeling:

from *Swimmers*

Oh, the swift plunge into the cool, green dark—
The windy waters rushing past me, through me;
Filled with a sense of some heroic lark,
Exulting in a vigor clean and roomy.
Swiftly I rose to meet the feline sea
That sprang upon me with a hundred claws,
And grappled, pulled me down and played with me.

LOUIS UNTERMEYER

Because all five senses usually work at the same time, they often take on each other's jobs: a face looks "sour," although it has no taste; a man feels "blue," although his mood can't be seen; a spice tastes "sharp," although it can't be touched; a red shirt is "loud," although it can't be heard. Writers purposely describe one sensation in terms of another, and you may want to make up some crossed senses too.

If the color orange could make a noise, it would proba-bly be a loud, smashing one, and if purple could join in, it would probably boom like a drum. What sort of sound do you suppose pale blue would make, or gray? Now close your eyes and touch. Touch the color pink, touch a scream, touch the smell of cigars. What does each one feel like? Or try imagining how a sound, a feeling, or a taste would look. What is the color of a whisper, a headache, a mouthful of vinegar?

So far, you've been exercising your senses one or two at a time. Now try to put them to work all at once. Choose a big scene—a snowy morning, a windy street, a school cafeteria, a rainy day—and look at it, listen to it, smell it, taste it, and feel it. Then write about it.

Suppose you choose a rainy day. What do you see on a rainy day that you don't see when it's dry? Outdoors you see the dripping and the wet, but what about indoors? You can tell it's raining just by seeing the umbrellas dripping in the doorway and the boot tracks across the floor. What else? What are the sounds of a rainy day? Sneakers squishing down the hall, for one, and water plopping on the lid of the trash can, for another. There are rainy-day smells, too: soggy grocery bags, wet rubber boots, woolen gloves drying on the radiator. There are rainy-day tastes: a rubbery raincoat collar against your lips, a soaking muffler in your mouth. And there are rainy-day feels: the towel rubbed against your face, the wet hair sticking to your neck, the wet socks clinging to your toes.

Now put all your observations, big and small, into words. Don't make a list; write out whole sentences. You needn't begin each sentence with "I see . . ." or "I hear . . ." Just tell what's there: "The water runs in rivers down the street, bubbling and boiling at the sewer mouth." "Quick droplets prick the stretched silk of my umbrella."

Here is how one poet "sensed" a field on a summer day and put his sensations into words:

The Waking

I strolled across
An open field;
The sun was out;
Heat was happy.

This way! This way!
The wren's throat shimmered,
Either to other,
The blossoms sang.

The stones sang,
The little ones did,
And flowers jumped
Like small goats.

A ragged fringe
Of daisies waved;
I wasn't alone
In a grove of apples.

Far in the wood
A nestling sighed;
The dew loosened
Its morning smells.

I came where the river
Ran over stones:
My ears knew
An early joy.

And all the waters
Of all the streams
Sang in my veins
That summer day.

THEODORE ROETHKE

If you had been standing in that field, you would have written an altogether different poem, because no two people experience the same thing the same way. Your senses, all together or one at a time, will show you a world that is not quite anyone else's world. It is up to you to show that world to the rest of us, putting perceptions that are your very own into words that are your very own.

PROSE

3

What Is Prose?

Nearly all the words you read in a day—in stories, letters, cookbooks, and comics; on billboards, menus, baseball cards, and shampoo bottles—are written in what is called *prose*. Maybe because there is so much of it around, prose is difficult to define. "Prose is not poetry" is what we usually hear.

But prose *is* something, too. If someone wrote down everything you said in a day—to your parents, to your friends, to your enemies, to your teachers, to your cat, to yourself—it would come out in a form that you would recognize as prose. Prose is the written form of natural speech. But with a difference.

When you speak, your words disappear immediately, like sparks in the air; when you write, your words last long after you've thought them up. When you speak, your listener is present, and you can tell by a nod or a blank stare whether you are making yourself clear; when you write, you receive no such signals. So, because words when put down on paper are meant to last and because they must communicate when you are not on hand to explain them, you choose them with greater care than when they are spoken. That, then, is what prose is: the words of natural speech written and chosen with care.

Prose is divided into two categories—the kind you make up from your imagination, which is *fiction*, and the kind you base on facts and ideas, which is *nonfiction.* Stories and novels are fiction. Biographies, letters, histories, and manuals—on how to fix a motorcycle, for example— are nonfiction. Sometimes the two overlap. When you report that Christopher Columbus discovered America in October 1492, that's nonfiction. When you quote him as saying, "Hey, man, dig that cool turf!" that's fiction.

FICTION

Everybody is a storyteller.

Everybody who tells anyone about anything that happened is a storyteller.

The three-year-old who tells his mother about the cat that climbed the fire escape across the street is a storyteller.

The caveman of long ago who returned from the hunt and told his friends about his kill was a storyteller.

And you, each time you come home from school and tell your family what happened on the playground, are a storyteller too.

The more exciting the event, the better the story.

But exciting events don't occur every day. Most of the time only so-so events occur. If a caveman killed only a couple of squirrels on a hunt, and if he told his friends his story, they would probably shrug and say, "So what?" But if he told them instead about the herds of imaginary antelope he'd encountered and the long-fanged monsters he'd fought off with his bare hands, his listeners might stop in their tracks and wait for more.

You, too, probably like to turn ordinary events into exciting adventures by adding details that were never there. "I stumbled on my way to school, but I didn't fall" may be an accurate account of an incident in your day, but it won't make your listeners' eyes widen. Like the caveman's friends, they are likely to say, "So what?" You begin to wish that you really had fallen, and broken a bone or two besides. And instead of having been on your way to school, you wish you had been on some rescue mission, with a life-saving drug instead of a paper-bag lunch in your hand. Maybe you will be bold enough to tell this story. Maybe not. Maybe you will realize that no one would believe it, so you simply turn it around in your mind where it becomes a daydream—a half wish, a secret boast, a would-be lie, a piece of make-believe.

In either case, that is how fiction is born.

Fiction begins when a real story stops and a daydream takes over.

Daydreams are not the time wasters you have probably been reprimanded for. Pay attention to them. Many of your daydreams begin with the unspoken question "What would it be like if . . . ?" What would it be like if you were a rock star or a hockey champion? What would it be like if you opened your locker door and a ghost stepped out? What would it be like if you were kidnaped? What would it be like if you were a balloonist? a witch? a turtle? a tube of toothpaste? What would it be like if you lived in a dungeon? an igloo? a cage in the zoo? a jar of peanut butter?

What *would* it be like? Next time you arouse yourself from a daydream, reach for a pencil and write down what went on in your mind. Make it into a story. Begin it, if you like, with "If I were . . ." Remember that every daydream is a story waiting to be told.

Not all the stories in your head are your very own. Some have already been told many times over. This does not mean that you cannot use them. Some basic story ideas remain unchanged from age to age, but adapt with the times as new characters and settings replace the old. The Superman of today's comic strip is a re-creation of the powerful hero of the ancient Greek myth. And the scheming villain on your favorite television serial is a modern-day version of the fairy tale's wicked witch. Any tale of long ago can be made into a new tale of today.

Your head is full of stories. Some are all yours, some are waiting to be made all yours. Some have been there a long time, some arrive fresh each day. All you have to do is recognize them and write them down.

NONFICTION

Nonfiction is just what its name suggests—it is not fiction. It is not myths or legends or fantasies or ghost stories. It is not stories that could be real but aren't. It is not stories at all. *Nonfiction* is that whole body of writing that is based on facts and ideas. The science assignments you write for school, your book reports, your letters to your grandmother, the notes you pass back and forth to your friends in class are all nonfiction.

Every category of writing seems to break down into smaller categories of its own. Nonfiction, a category of prose, can be divided into smaller groups, and, of course, as with everything else that gets separated and labeled, many areas overlap so that it is hard to decide where to place what. Some nonfiction is based entirely on facts. Reports on the structure of the atom or instructions for making clam chowder fall into this category. Some nonfiction is based on ideas and feelings. Essays on what it's like to ski down a mountain, or why kids should get into the movies free, belong here. So do letters telling how homesick you are. Some nonfiction includes both facts and ideas. Book reports in which you tell both what the book is about and how you liked it belong in this category.

4

Myths

Imagine yourself living at a time, centuries and centuries ago, when your understanding of the world around you is based only on what your eyes and ears tell you. No one has yet charted the seas, measured the stars, traveled the globe—or even figured out that there *is* a globe—examined a cell, or mined the earth. What would you know?

By day a blaze of light appears and moves across the sky from edge to edge until it slips without a splash into the sea. Enormous puffs of smoke that sail like phantom boats above the earth change shape, collide, move on. By night the sky, now black and still, is all abloom with tiny points of light. And stealthily, a silver glow, at times a slender spiderleg, at times a giant coin, begins its quiet climb and hangs itself upon some unseen hook.

Light and dark, light and dark. What makes it change? The sky, pale blue the day before, turns gray and mean, and tiny drops of water fall. Or stinging flakes of white drop down and dress the trees with crowns and sleeves. What makes things change? What makes them move?

You will already have noticed that some things move and change because they are alive. Birds fly because they are alive, horses gallop, fish swim, insects crawl, snakes slither, and people walk and run because they are alive. Maybe the sun is alive and flies across the sky like a bird? Maybe the moon is alive and grows and shrinks like a blossom? Maybe the clouds are alive and swim through the sky like fish?

You will also have noticed that some things move and change because living beings make them do so. When you pick up a stone and swing your arm, the stone sails through the air. When you blow on a feather, it flies away; when you stir a pond, it bubbles and heaves; and when you shake a tree, leaves fall to the ground. Maybe some living being is rolling the sun across the sky, or throwing it or kicking it or playing catch with it or carrying it around. Maybe some living being is lighting the stars, nibbling at the moon, sprinkling rain, dropping hailstones, scattering snow, stirring the seas, and cracking the sky. Maybe some living being warms the ground and colors it green, while another hardens it and colors it brown. Maybe some living being bangs a hidden gong that smashes the air when it rains, and another trails a colored scarf across the sky when all the noise has stopped. But who?

The ancient Egyptians imagined these beings to be spirits in monstrous shapes—strange creatures, one with the body of a man, perhaps, and the head of a bird, another with the head of a woman on the body of a cat. They were thought to inhabit the rivers, deserts, and towns, and they were worshiped and feared by human beings.

The American Indians imagined a spiritual world

filled with creatures close to the earth—talking animals, underground fairies, giants, dwarfs, and a whole community of Little People who wore invisible moccasins and traveled about in winged canoes.

The early Africans assigned magical powers not only to deities but to their own ancestors as well and worshiped them all equally.

But the Greeks added something new. Their gods and goddesses, instead of appearing in the shape of animals or semihumans, were modeled entirely on the human form. They were conceived in the image of man and woman, but stronger, more beautiful, more wonderfully built. Their bodies were like those of the ancient Greek statues you see in museums today. Greek gods and goddesses behaved very much like men and women, too. They grew angry and jealous, selfish and spiteful. They would go off and sulk. But they possessed powers that humans could only long for. Like the ocean, the sky, the earth, the moon, and the sun that they ruled, gods and goddesses lived forever. They were immortal. What's more, they held the destiny of mortal men and women in their hands. They might cover the earth with floods or drought and fill the sky with sunlight or storms. They might, in a moment of anger, transform an impudent girl into a quivering insect or a conceited boy into a nodding flower.

The early Romans took over the Greek family of gods and goddesses and gave them Roman names, making changes here and there to suit their own needs.

The mythmakers of long ago provided explanations

for grand things and for lowly things as well. Why did the sun travel across the sky? The Egyptians told of Ra, the sun god, sailing with it in a boat. The Greeks told of Apollo, *their* sun god, riding a chariot from east to west with the sun on his head, like a crown. Why did spiders spin? The Greeks told of Arachne, the skillful weaver, who dared challenge Athena, goddess of handicrafts, to a weaving competition and who was doomed to weave for all eternity in the form of a crawling, eight-legged creature. Why do woodpeckers peck? The American Indians told of a selfish woman who refused to offer her home-baked bread to the Great Spirit and was forced to dig her food out of trees with a beak forever.

If you had been living long ago, how would you have explained the journey of the sun across the sky? Was the sun carried or worn, or was it tossed across the sky like a flaming volleyball, and if so, by whom? A myth that explains why something happens is called a *pourquoi myth*. *Pourquoi* (pronounced "poor-KWAH") is the French word for *why*. You can get ideas for your *pourquoi* myth just by looking outside. Why does the robin cover his chest with an orange bib? Why does the dandelion's hair turn from yellow to white? Why does a woodpecker wear a red beret wherever he goes? You can get ideas from the zoo. Why does the porcupine keep a clutch of hat pins in his back? Why does the raccoon hide behind a black mask? Why does the kangaroo keep babies instead of loose change in her pocket?

Begin your myth like this: once, long, long ago there were no waves in the ocean. Or: birds had no wings; monkeys had no tails; bees had no sting; there were no flowers or snakes or rainbows. How did all these things come to be? Who put them there? Why? If you are familiar with Greek gods and goddesses, put some of them into your story. Or you may want to make up a whole new set of gods and goddesses of your own. You may, if you like, leave gods out of your story altogether and put in talking birds and animals, as the American Indians and Africans did.

Mythology explained more than the mysteries of the natural world. Through mythology people also sought reasons for the uncertainties of their luck. One family's crops withered and died while their neighbors' flourished. One house was struck by lightning while another was spared. An avalanche of rocks destroyed one herd of cattle and left another untouched. How come? Maybe the spirits who controlled the earth and the sky used their powers also to punish and reward ordinary human beings. Myths from all civilizations deal with the antics of gods and goddesses rewarding people for behaving themselves properly and punishing them for not.

Think of all the things you might do if you were a god or goddess for one day with unlimited powers to reward or punish. Instead of stamping your foot and slamming the door, you could destroy entire neighborhoods with a barrage of thunderbolts. You could transform your enemy into a cow. You could cast a whole gang of enemies into the sky and fix them there permanently as stars.

You could flood the school basement. What would you do?

Gods and goddesses frequently disguised themselves to test the loyalty of ordinary mortals. They would turn up on somebody's doorstep dressed as beggars or travelers from some distant land and would either reward or punish their hosts according to the extent of their hospitality. If you had this power to punish or reward, how would you use it? Or suppose, instead, that a god or goddess in disguise visited you. What if a Halloween trick-or-treater turned out to be a god or goddess testing your loyalty. How do you think you would feel when you found out?

Mythology, and especially Greek mythology, survived long after people stopped believing in its gods and goddesses. To this day, we read and reread these ancient tales and use their themes in new tales of our own. Many modern stories are really Greek myths in disguise. The musical show *My Fair Lady,* adapted from a play by George Bernard Shaw, is about a poor London girl who is made into an elegant lady by a scholar who trains her to improve her speech and manners. He then falls in love with her. The story is a modern version of the Greek myth about Pygmalion, a sculptor who falls in love with the statue of a beautiful woman he has fashioned out of a block of stone.

There are many ancient myths whose characters can be dressed in modern clothes and set in modern surroundings, but whose essential story remains unchanged. Read the following myth. Then rewrite it so that it takes place in your own neighborhood with characters just like the people you meet every day.

Phaëthon

Phaëthon was the son of Apollo, the god who each day drove a chariot across the sky with the flaming sun upon his head. Phaëthon liked to boast to his schoolmates that he was the son of a god, but no one believed him, and he was laughed at and taunted. One day he asked his mother, the sea nymph Clymene, how he might prove to his friends that he was the son of the sun god. "Go to your father," she advised, "and ask him to give you the proof you need."

Immediately, Phaëthon set out for the palace in the east where Apollo, the sun resting on his head, readied his horses and chariot for his daily journey across the sky. "Father," said the boy, standing before Apollo's throne, "I have come to ask you to give me proof that I am your son, so that my friends will no longer make fun of me." "Ask me what you will," his father replied, "and you shall have what you wish." Phaëthon's reply was swift. "I want to drive the sun chariot across the sky for one day," he said.

Apollo was greatly alarmed at his son's request, for it took great skill and experience to lead the horses through the heavens. Immediately he regretted his offer, but he would not go back on his word, and reluctantly he granted Phaëthon his wish. "It is a very dangerous journey," he warned, "for the horses are fast and wild. You must take care not to drive them too high or you will scorch the home of the gods. And you must not drive them too low or you will set the earth on fire."

But Phaëthon was impatient and did not listen to his father. Eagerly he waited as his father placed the brilliant ball of fire on his head, and then he mounted the chariot and grasped the reins. As soon as they were outside the palace gates, the horses sensed that they were being guided by strange hands. They began to race wildly from side to side and then to climb higher and higher in the sky. Frantically, Phaëthon tried to rein them in, but he succeeded only in driving them closer to earth. Soon the mountains began to burn and then the forests and fields, until the whole earth was in flames.

"Save us, O Zeus!" people cried to the king of the gods. "Save us!" they cried from the fields and the mountains and the riverbanks. And Zeus, looking down from his dwelling place on Mount Olympus and seeing the earth rapidly being destroyed in fire, hurled a thunderbolt at Phaëthon. The young boy fell from his seat on the chariot and plunged down, down, down into the river below, where his bones rest to this day.

For a start, you will want to give Phaëthon a new name. If you like, you can change him into a girl. Next, you can put him or her in a school very much like your own school, with classmates very much like yours. What could take the place of the chariot? A brand-new Cadillac? Give it a try.

5

Hero Tales and Tall Tales

The ancient myths not only told of powerful gods and goddesses; they told of powerful men and women as well—of heroes and heroines with greater strength, greater courage, or greater wit than most ordinary mortals could hope to attain.

Every age has had its heroes and heroines, real and made up, who have served as the embodiment of all the dreams and ambitions of an entire culture. The ancient Jews had their Samson, who tore apart a lion with his bare hands and slew a thousand men with the jawbone of an ass. The English had their King Arthur and their Robin Hood. The French had their Joan of Arc, who led a small army to victory in a battle against the English. And the Americans had their Davy Crockett, the frontiersman, and Paul Bunyan, the lumberjack.

The Greeks had their Hercules. Hercules was probably the greatest hero of all time. So strong was he that the gods called on him to help them out in their battle against the Giants, and they treated him as their equal, although he belonged to the world of human beings.

When he was a baby in his cradle he strangled two venomous serpents with his bare hands. As a penance for
having killed his wife and children in a moment of mad-
ness, he undertook twelve tasks, all beyond the capabili-
ties of even the strongest of ordinary men. They were
known as the "Labors of Hercules," and most of them
required the slaying or capture of violent, powerful monsters—a lion with flesh so hard no weapon could pene-
trate it, a nine-headed creature that would grow two new
heads whenever one was severed, a golden-horned stag,
a giant boar, an enormous swarm of man-eating birds, a
savage bull, a three-headed dog. All of these tasks Hercules accomplished by his strength alone, for he was not
a clever man.

Everybody has a hero. At one time or another, there's
somebody around, somebody older and stronger,
maybe, whom you wish you could be like. Somebody
sensational on the ball field or at the piano or on the
skating rink. The less certain you are of your own abilities, the more likely you are to admire those abilities in
someone else. If you don't have a hero at hand, you
might make one up—somebody who can score all the
goals you wish you could score or zip through all the
sonatas you wish you could play. A hero is a person you
wish you might be. Sometimes a hero is real, sometimes
made up, sometimes both. Real people can never be as
wonderful as their fans would like, and so they're often
made out to be better than they are. There really was a
frontiersman named Davy Crockett and he really was an
excellent shot, but he didn't have all the adventures you

have heard about. No one could have. Chances are there really was an Arthur who was a military chieftain of some sort, but he was never made king, and he never removed a sword from a stone, as the legend says he did.

The difference between the tale of Davy Crockett and the tale of Hercules is the difference between a legend and a myth. A legend is based on some historical fact, a real person or a real event, that has been exaggerated and distorted until it takes on the characteristics of fantasy. A myth is fantasy to begin with and has no historical basis at all.

A hero myth in the tradition of the ancient Greek tales is usually about a battle between a human being and a monster. Someone has been ordered by an angry god to slay a creature no mortal has yet been able to approach. Sometimes the hero performs this task using strength or wits alone. Sometimes luck wins the day. Just as often a friendly god or goddess helps out.

To write a hero myth of your own, you might make up the monster first and then create the hero to slay it. Make your monster truly monstrous. Give it claws filled with venom or wings with vicious thorns, a beak like the blade of a knife, an eye whose fire burns holes in human flesh, a tail that strangles like a rope, scales of iron, or nails of lead. Your monster can be mostly human or mostly beast. It can wage its battles alone or it can be part of a trio—or a swarm—of monsters just like it.

Your hero can be superstrong or supersmart or super-lucky. Make him or her a good match for the monster, but not too good. The battle should be a difficult one.

You might want to add some gods and goddesses of your own to your story, some to order the hero around and others to offer help. The friendly ones can give tips. (The monster falls asleep every time it takes a bath, or the monster has a weakness for jelly beans.) They can also slip your hero weapons, like double-bladed hatchets, just right for hacking through iron scales.

Heroes reflect those qualities that are valued most by the culture in which they are born. The monster-slaying hero of the Greek myth gave way, in time, to the man-slaying hero of the medieval legend. Civilizations engaged in constant warfare gave rise to figures who were heroes on the battlefield. King Arthur of Britain was a hero of war and, with the aid both of superhuman strength and magic powers, was able to slay thousands of men in battle. Industrial societies produce worker heroes like John Henry, the steel-driving man from West Virginia, who could hammer a spike faster than a steam-driven machine.

No matter how strong men and women may be, there are still boulders they cannot budge, waters they cannot stay, beasts they cannot crush, and football passes they cannot catch. Yet necessity demands that they try. Sometimes they are successful; often they fail. In their frustration, they fulfill their goals in wishes and dreams. The teller of a hero tale is saying, "I wish I could do that," and the listener nods in agreement.

People who work together create heroes together.

Cowboys create cowboy heroes. Sailors create sailor heroes. Pioneers create pioneer heroes. How about creating a kid hero? Every school or neighborhood needs a good kid hero, someone who can hang the local big shot by a belt loop from the branch of a tree. Make your kid hero superstrong, superwise, supertall, and superbrave, but still a kid. Write about what your Super-kid does. Think up a good enemy for your kid hero to crush and let the battle begin.

Suppose *you* were the Superkid of your town or neighborhood. You are so strong you can knock down the movie house with a few swift kicks, and you can snuff out a fire with a flick of your finger. You are so tall you strap buses on your feet for roller skates and you can rest your chin on the third-story windowsill. Every time a disaster hits, you come along and save the town. What are some good disasters? Floods, blizzards, fires, and hurricanes could keep you busy. So could an enemy invasion. How about some not-so-real disasters? What if there were an invasion of earthworms? What if millions of earthworms began slithering into the streets, through the basement windows, up the stairs, and into everybody's living room? You are Superkid, and everyone turns to you to dry them up or sweep them out or gather them in your massive fists and throw them into the sea. What will you do? Write about it.

Many present-day heroes perform their deeds in the pages of comic books. Hercules would have been jealous of Superman's steel skin, X-ray vision, and wingless flight. You can make up a comic-strip hero of your own. Instead of drawing cartoon characters who speak through bubbles over their heads, write out your hero's adventures as you would any other story. Your hero doesn't have to have a great many extraordinary abilities. One will do. How about someone who has a thirty-foot arm that, on command, unrolls like a garden hose? What are some useful things someone might do with such an arm? Retrieve lost balls and skate keys from storm sewers? Untangle kites from telephone poles and rescue treed cats? Fish without a rod, write on the blackboard from the back of the room, or borrow a math book from the kid next door without moving from the living-room sofa?

Every hero has a deed to perform, either an enemy to defeat or a victim to rescue. Once you have made up a hero with special talent, think up a situation that will put those talents to use. A thirty-foot arm can reach through a window and tie a spy to the radiator or pluck papers from secret files. It can also lift a frozen skater out of a hole in the pond.

Hero stories often take the form of the tall tale. A tall tale is a lie you know no one will believe. It is a wild exaggeration. Many tall tales arose in work camps. Sitting around in bunkhouses after a day of exhausting labor, cowpunchers, railroad workers, or loggers would entertain one another with outrageous adventures of

heroes bigger, stronger, faster, and hungrier than anyone alive. They were meant to be absurd, and no one
took them seriously.

Unlike the comic strip or the old-time hero tale, the tall
tale does not have much of a plot. It is often simply
descriptive. When Paul Bunyan, the lumberjack favorite
of loggers in northern America, was a baby, so the story
goes, he was so big he kicked down four square miles of
trees every time he had a stomachache. Too big for a
cradle, he was anchored out at sea in the largest boat
ever built, and whole villages were wiped out whenever
he stirred in his sleep. He ate seventy-five buckets of
porridge a day, and his coat had wheelbarrow wheels for
buttons. A few years later, he could run so fast that once
when he shot at a deer five miles away, he reached the
animal before the bullet did and he got a seat full of lead.
By the time he was full grown, his nose was the size of
a leg of lamb, his beard had to be combed with a pine
tree, and a ten-gallon pail would have been lost in his
yawning mouth.

Here are the beginnings of some tall tales you can
write yourself:

I once knew a man who was so tall he . . .
There once was a woman who could run so fast she . . .
Once there was a baby who was so strong she . . .
The hungriest man I ever saw once ate . . .

Your tall tale can simply be one exaggeration after
another. Like this:

Once there was a man who was so tall he had to keep a tin pail over his head to keep the sun from frizzing his hair. Whenever he wanted to go anywhere, he'd simply grab hold of his ankles and roll like a doughnut. He had an awful time stopping eagles from building nests in his back pocket, and once his left ear was nipped by the wing of a passing airplane.

Or a tall tale can be built around a single incident:

Once there was a girl who could blow bubble-gum bubbles so big that one day when she was sitting in her classroom she blew the walls of the school down, and children, desks, chalk, teachers, books, and papers were scattered so far and wide it took three weeks to find them all, and one boy hasn't been found yet.

Tall tales aren't always about tall or strong people. They can be about little people, too: "There was a woman who was so small she could tuck herself into the toe of her sock, and a man who was so skinny he once sipped himself up through a straw when he was having a milk shake."

Some tall tales are not about people at all. They're about cats or pigs or horses or ears of corn or mosquitoes: "Once there was a swarm of mosquitoes so thick a man thought it was a blanket and he covered his horse with it for the night. The last he saw of his horse, it was being carried off through the air at thirty miles an hour." And "Once there was a pig that was so thin someone pasted it into a scrapbook by mistake."

Tall tales can be about the cold or the fog or the rain:

"Once it was so cold a whole row of birds perched on somebody's frozen breath and were stuck there for three weeks, when it finally thawed and they all fell on their heads." And "Once the fog was so thick a woman bumped her head on it and raised a lump three inches in diameter." And "Once it rained so hard all the fish drowned."

Write a tall tale without people. Write about the day it was so cold the sun refused to go outside or about the dog who ran so fast it left its ears behind. Write about the bolt of lightning that zigzagged across the street, knocking all the houses down, and then zigzagged back, picking them all up again. Write about the grass that grew so tall that . . . what?

Such a story may not at first seem like a hero tale. But every hero tale is an exaggeration. The hero is exaggerated, and so is the enemy. In some tall tales it is the foe alone—the cold, the fog, the swarm of mosquitoes—that we hear of, while the hero gets left behind. But for every snowflake the size of a lump of coal, for every mosquito the size of a cow, there is, somewhere, an unmentioned hero who has seen it and survived to tell about it.

6

Fantasy
Fairy Tales, Ghost Stories, Science Fiction

All fiction is make-believe, but some kinds are more make-believe than others. A story about a boy who finds a million dollars' worth of baseball cards hidden in a laundry bag may never actually have taken place, and probably never will, but it *could* have happened. A story about a princess who is transformed by a fairy into a bantam hen could never have happened at all. It is a fantasy. The ancient myth was a fantasy in which gods, goddesses, and monsters provided the elements of magic that lifted it from the world of the real to the world of the unreal. But as men and women gained control over and understanding of their surroundings, their need to believe in a complicated system of deities diminished. With their changing beliefs came a change in the storyteller's treasury of make-believe figures. Gods and goddesses gave way to other, less powerful dealers in magic and enchantment.

FAIRY TALES

The most familiar magic characters belong to the unorganized, often ill-mannered crowd of creatures we meet in the fairy tale—witches, sorcerers, leprechauns, elves, fairies, gnomes, goblins, dwarfs, genies, pixies, imps, trolls, brownies, wizards, kobolds, and sprites. Like their ancestor gods and goddesses, these new wielders of magic were possessed of an unending supply of wondrous tricks and an unending urge to use them. They operated, however, on a smaller scale. They could sew up a batch of shoes for a sleeping cobbler, if the mood so struck them, or they could put an entire kingdom to sleep for a hundred years, but the really big jobs—managing the ocean and the sky and the changing earth—were now left to unseen forces of nature.

While the ancient gods usually accomplished their wonders with their bare hands only, most members of the fairy-tale crowd came equipped with special tools of the trade. They waved wands, uttered spells, twisted rings, rubbed lamps, stirred potions, or sprinkled powders. The results, however, were the same. Whether you were changed into a bull by an unarmed god or into a frog by a wand-waving sorcerer, the inconvenience to your life was the same, and storytellers throughout the ages have understood this.

Fantasy creatures take many forms, human and not quite human. Some have characteristics that identify them right away. If you were to meet up with an elf or a witch in the subway, you would recognize it instantly for what it was. Others, like Mary Poppins, in a modern fairy tale, look and dress like everyone else, and it isn't until they start sliding up stair rails or taking off on kite tails that you begin to suspect their true character.

The first thing you might do in writing a fairy tale of your own is pick a magic character. Then assign to it some special powers. A fairy's specialty usually lies in the area of transformation. There is no end of transformations a skillful fairy, good-tempered or bad, can bring about. She can turn a lovely prince into a pig or a beautiful girl into an old hag. Or the other way around. She can change a scattering of pebbles into an armload of shining gold or a hut into a gleaming palace. She can reduce a full-grown man to the size of a big toe or enlarge a housefly to the size of a gymnasium. Suppose that in a moment of bad temper she chose to turn you into an octopus and then, out of carelessness, forgot to turn you back again. Try to imagine that. What would your school day be like? How about your evening at the dinner table or your trip with your mother to the shoe store? Write a story about somebody who is transformed by a fairy into something altogether inappropriate and who has to continue to lead his former life.

Maybe, instead of writing about everyday goblins and elves, you would like to create an entirely new creature of your own. Give her the antennae of a bee, if you like, or tiny bird wings on her wrists. Make her ten inches tall or ten feet, good-natured or vile, clever or bumbling.

Make her the only one of her kind or a member of an entire regiment. Give her a name and something to do. You will probably find that what she does is not unlike what the heroes of your hero stories did or the gods and goddesses of your myths: she will perform miracles. But instead of relying on unnatural strength or divine powers, she will make use of her private store of magic gifts.

Now create a familiar person, the sort you see every day—a teacher, a bus driver, a zookeeper—and give him or her one secret, magic power. Suppose a teacher could lead her entire class through the blackboard and into a hidden kingdom. Suppose a bus driver could fly his bus back to the eighteenth century. Suppose a zookeeper could turn all the animals, for one night out of the year, into human beings. Write a story telling what your not-so-ordinary character would do with the secret power you have chosen. Put yourself in the story, if you like, or let it all happen to somebody else.

Your magic story needn't be about magic people. It can be about magic *things.* What if you found a magic key on the pavement in front of your house one night? You knew it was magic by the way it sparkled. What kind of magic might it possess? It might have a kind of overall power, like a wand, that would grant you any wish you made, or it could have more specific powers. It might open any door in the world, or it might open only one. Which one? What would lie on the other side? The key might transform the room behind any door it opened. How? How might it transform your own room? It might be a special kind of key—a car key, maybe, that enables your car to take you wherever you wish.

What if, instead of a magic key, you found a magic shell that whispered secrets from far away or a rocking chair that rocked you into the past? A kite that flew you to a land no one had ever seen before or a painting that opened up and let you in? What would a magic pencil do? A magic baseball bat? Magic eyeglasses? A magic mirror? Pick any five objects in your house or in your classroom and make them magic. Write a story about what each one might do.

GHOST STORIES

Another regular member of the world of fantasy is the ghost. We meet ghosts in various forms and in different surroundings, but their purpose is nearly always the same—to scare. Often they accomplish this by not appearing at all; a gust of chill air passing through a bedroom is evidence enough that one is present. So is a melody suddenly playing itself on the keys of a piano in an empty parlor.

Suppose a ghost took up residence in your living room. You couldn't see it, but you could see what it was doing. Without warning, the rocking chair would be set in motion, and the curtain at the closed window would ripple. Pages of magazines would turn, one after another, and lamps would brighten and dim. A record would spin on the phonograph, and the closet door would creak open and shut. The cobweb across the lampshade would silently shatter, and the fruit on the table would roll onto the floor. Suppose the ghost brought a pal along, and they became rowdy. They might decide to play catch with the sofa pillows and shuffle-board with the ashtrays. What would that sound like from the next room? What would you see when you walked into the middle of such a scene? Write a story about it.

Now tell your story from the point of view of the ghosts. Suppose you and your ghost family set up house-keeping in an apartment in the middle of a big city. How would you keep your presence a secret? Suppose you were part of a whole class of early colonial ghosts, teacher and all, who took over a schoolroom and con-ducted lessons every night. What would you write on the board? Where would you hide during the day? Behind the window shades? In an empty drawer? Among the coats? What would you think of the classes going on during the day?

Not all ghosts are disagreeable. Some settle in com-fortably with a family of their choosing, join in amiably in all their games and picnics, and turn out to be not only acceptable but useful. You might write about a family ghost who helps out with the housework and looks after the kids. What might the neighbors make of parents who go out and leave the children without a visible baby-sitter?

Stories in which readers don't know until the last mo-ment that they are dealing with a ghost can often be the most frightening of all. Write about a stranger whose mysterious dress and behavior are explained only at the very end when it is revealed that she is paying an annual call to the scene of her death.

Ghost stories don't have to be about ghosts at all. They can be about ghostly things: a television set that foretells death, a mirror that reveals scary scenes of the past, a room whose furnishings suddenly change one night to match those of a long-dead ancestor. Pick an article of furniture in your house and imagine that it is haunted. It belonged to someone who died long ago, and every now and then it behaves as though its owner has returned. What does it do?

SCIENCE FICTION

Science fiction is the fantasy of modern times. It is a fairy tale with machines instead of wands, robots instead of sorcerers, spaceships instead of flying carpets, computer printouts instead of talking mirrors. It is fantasy with technology. Sometimes, as it turns out, it isn't fantasy at all, but an accurate forecast of scientific development to come. The rocket ships of the twentieth century were foretold in the science fantasies of the nineteenth century.

Not that the author of such a fantasy intended such an outcome. He or she probably sat down and asked a question beginning "What if . . . ?" and let his or her mind wander off into endless paths of improbabilities. What if everyone could put on aluminum skin? What if there were a real world inside a mirror? What if there were somebody just like you with parents just like yours living in a house just like the one you live in, all on another planet? What if there were a machine that enabled people to read one another's minds? Eyeglasses that let you see behind closed doors? A ship that moved faster than the speed of light? A machine that did your homework?

What *if* there were a machine that did your homework? Everybody's homework, even? What if a calculator did all your math, a reading machine did all your reading, a typewriter did all your reports? What would you do yourself? What would it be like not needing to read or write at all? What if no one in the whole world needed to read or write? What if everyone forgot how? How would your neighborhood change? What would your school day be like? Would there *be* a school day? What if other machines brushed your teeth, made your bed, washed your face, combed your hair, buttoned your shirt, tied your sneakers, fed you your cornflakes, carried you to the ball field, pitched balls at you, batted them, ran around the bases, and then cheered you as they slid home? What if there was nothing left to do at all, not even sleep, because a machine took care of that too? What if? There's a little good and often a lot of bad in the unlimited power of any machine, and science fiction usually explores both.

Because one kind of fantasy is often an adaptation of another, you might want to borrow an idea or two for your science fiction from a fairy tale or a Greek myth. Do you remember Jack the Giant Killer? Jack's mother, in a fit of anger, threw a handful of seemingly worthless beans out the window and the next morning found a stalk reaching to the sky. At its top, as her son soon learned, stood a giant's kingdom. What if a scientist could develop a wonder seed that produced cities, instead of bean stalks in the air? What if they kept growing and growing? What if *you* were that scientist? What kind of seed would you perfect? Suppose one plant-city declared war on another plant-city. What sorts of weapons might they use against each other?

Pandora, according to Greek mythology, was the first woman to be created on earth. She was given a sealed casket by Zeus, king of the gods, who cautioned her never to lift its lid. He knew full well that she would ignore his warning, and she did. Overcome one day by curiosity, she pried open the box and in so doing released its contents—a horrifying assortment of miseries, evils, and ailments that have assaulted the human race ever since. With a little bit of tinkering and updating here and there, this story can be changed into a science-fiction account of a laboratory assistant, maybe, who was given a tightly stoppered test tube and warned never to unseal it. What might have happened when he or she gave in to curiosity and ignored the warning?

You don't have to be a scientist to write science fiction. It isn't necessary to explain the technology of your make-believe machine or to describe the electronic principles behind its operation. You don't have to create a make-believe machine at all. You can use a real one and

make it go haywire. And you don't have to understand
how that one works either. Any familiar machine will do.
Pick one from around the house—a television, say—and
make it more amazing than anything of its kind. Twist
one of its dials, and there on the screen is your uncle
brushing his teeth five hundred miles away. Twist another and a gang of hostile Martians appears, loading a
swarm of deadly butterflies into a spaceship and discussing plans to release them over New York City. Now twist
a third and watch yourself ten years from now with a
beard or high heels. Here are some other ordinary machines that might take on new and fantastic properties
with some help from your imagination: a telephone, a
bicycle, a bulldozer, a waffle iron, a buzz saw, a snow
blower, a vacuum cleaner.

Many of the fantasies in the storybooks of your early
years probably don't fit into any of these categories, but
they are fantasies nevertheless. All those tales where animals sit around in living rooms wearing bathrobes and
slippers, reading the newspaper, and discussing tomorrow's outing are fantasies. So are all those talking-toy
stories where the inhabitants of the toyshop come to life
each night and raise a ruckus. What if all the things in
your room came to life while you were away at school?
Not just the dolls and stuffed bears, but your baseball bat
and glove, your ballpoint pen, your shoes, even your
bed. What would go on? Would they talk about you?
Would they mess up your room? How? Write about it.

Whatever form of fantasy you choose to write—science fiction, fairy tale, ghost story, or myth—let your

imagination take your story as far away from the real world as it chooses to go. Your imagination, with its ability to change reality into fantasy in an instant, is the greatest magician of them all. Sit back and watch it perform.

7

People
Characters and Dialogue

While ghosts, animals, robots, gods, superheroes, and talking dolls may be the principal characters of many tales, it is people—real, live, flesh-and-blood human beings—whom we meet in the overwhelming majority of the stories we read from day to day.

And when we meet them, we want to get to know them. How do they look, first of all, and what are they like—are they nice, mean, grouchy, sloppy, or dumb? And what do they have to say?

To create real, live characters, the kind your readers can get to know, it is best to pay attention to real, live people. All kinds of people—those you know and those you don't, those you see every day in your living room and classroom and those you just brush by on your way to school.

HOW PEOPLE LOOK   Pick out someone you can look at for a while and examine him or her with care. What is he or she wearing? Take a good look, not just a glance that shows you jeans and a jacket. Look at the valentine patch on the seat of the jeans and the tear at the hem of each leg. Look at the broken laces on the sneakers and the pictures inked on each toe. Look at the pencil pocket on the sleeve of the jacket and the zipper that opens halfway down the front. Look at the woolen cap with the pompon on top and the name PEPSI-COLA knitted in blue and red around the crown.

What kind of features does he or she have? Small eyes or large, sharp nose or flat, round chin or pointy, fat cheeks or saggy? How about skin? Hair? Ears?

Look at his or her hands. Do they have big knuckles, lots of freckles, bulging veins, wrinkles? Are the finger-nails bitten, jagged, dirty, sharp, or polished, and is there a little crescent moon at the base of each nail?

What is his or her shape? Tall and skinny, like a clothespole? Short and squat, like a fire hydrant? Roly-poly, like a beach ball?

By now you will be ready to compose a written portrait that will show in words what a painting might show in oils. Your subject won't see what you've written, so you don't have to be complimentary. You may say things like "His throat bulged out of his collar like a frog's," if that's the way he looks to you, or "His mouth worked like a cow's," or "Her hair was matted like an old bathmat."

If you have chosen someone you and your friends know well, read your description aloud and see if anyone can guess whom it's about. Don't be discouraged if not too many can. You will have studied your subject more carefully than they.

Here's another guessing game to play with a friend: in

newspapers or magazines find pictures of ten girls or ten
boys or ten men or ten women. Put them in a row where
you can both see them. Choose one face to describe, but
don't tell each other your choices. Describe the face in
writing, picking out characteristics that don't appear on
any other face, and read your descriptions aloud. See if
you can each guess which face the other chose. The more
careful the description, the easier it will be to guess.

Now write a portrait of someone you've never seen.
Make up a character out of your head—boy or girl, man
or woman. Choose a name and describe your character's
appearance—big or small, fat or thin. Give your character something to wear. Your mind contains an unlimited
wardrobe from which to choose. Pick from it something
neat or sloppy, elegant or beat up. Describe it with as
much detail as you did the clothing of real people, down
to the threads on the hems of the jeans.

Now give your character a face. It won't do to say, "Mr.
Porter was funny-looking," or "Alyssa was cute." Readers want to know more than that. What makes Mr. Porter's face funny-looking? His oversized ears? His big
teeth? Say that. Describe his eyes, too, and his nose and
mouth. Describe his hair, his skin, his hands, and his feet.
Describe him so carefully that if your reader were to
meet him on the street, he'd recognize him right away.

WHAT PEOPLE DO   When you meet new friends, you do,
of course, check out their clothes and faces, but you want
to know more about them than just that. You want to
know what they're *like*. What do they do? How do they

do it? What do they say? Readers want to know the same things about characters in stories.

The best way to describe how a character does something is to watch a real person do it first. As a beginning, go outside and watch some people walk down the street. Look at their feet. Do their toes point in or out? Do they take little steps or big ones? Now look at their hands. Are they clasped, swinging, or hanging down straight? How about their shoulders, their chins, and their heads? People have different walks for different kinds of weather. How do they walk in the wind? In the snow? In the rain? When it's broiling hot or bitterly cold? Very often people reveal how they feel about themselves by the way they walk. Look over the following list of characters. How do you think each one would walk down the street? Describe two or three in writing.

Monica was always daydreaming.
Louie thought he was a big shot.
Jonathan was scared of everything.
Caroline thought nobody liked her.
Mrs. Oleson was fussy.

How many different ways do people sit? Look around your classroom and find out. Somebody probably has his feet wrapped around his chair legs, and somebody else has probably tipped her chair so far back that at any moment it will crash to the floor. Very likely somebody is resting his chin on his desk; somebody's feet are stretched out in the aisle; somebody is sitting on one foot; somebody's neck is draped over the back of her chair; somebody is about to slip off the front edge of his chair; somebody's arms are clasped behind his head; somebody's arms are hanging, baboon style, at her side; somebody is warming his hands under his thighs; and somebody is gripping the sides of her seat as though it were about to fly away. How about you? How are you sitting?

It is a good idea to pay attention to how you do things yourself. There are, in fact, some activities that you can observe better in yourself than in anyone else. Eating an ice-cream cone, for example. How do you go about that? Do you begin with a large bite off the top and then nibble around the edges, or do you sweep your tongue around the entire scoop in ascending spirals? Do you chew the cone along with the ice cream, or do you save it for last? Do you snip off the tip of the cone and let the melted ice cream trickle into your mouth, or do you simply throw it away when the ice cream is gone?

What do you do with a Life Saver? Bite smack into it or suck on it until it becomes a sliver-thin ring you can slip your tongue through? Do you cram a whole bagful of peanuts into your mouth and enjoy an all-out, bang-up peanut experience, or do you nip at them one at a time, daintily sucking the salt off, to make them last? Do you stop up a drinking straw with your tongue so that the liquid remains in vertical suspension, or do you blow up a volcano of bubbles at the bottom of the glass? Or first one and then the other?

Try to remember how you put on a pullover sweater.

Do you put your arms through the sleeves first, or do you first pull it over your head? Or do you let the whole thing hang over your face like a lampshade while you sort out the sleeves and the neck hole all at once? How do you enter a revolving door? By standing outside for five minutes, pumping your body back and forth, readying yourself for the jump? Do you usually end up in the wrong wedge, your toes on the heels of someone in front of you? Do you spin around in it seven or eight times before you gain the courage to leap out? Do you get out where you got on instead of where you meant to get off?

Become a snoop. Snoop on other people, and snoop on yourself. Then, if any of the characters in your stories should happen to take a walk, sit in a chair, eat an ice-cream cone, put on a sweater, or enter a revolving door, you will know exactly how to make them go about it.

PEOPLE AT WORK Now watch people work. There's bound to be somebody in your neighborhood performing some sort of task—painting a room, moving furniture, mowing a lawn, cutting hair, plowing a field. Get your notebook and pen and watch what he or she does. You may not even have to go outside. Watch your mother or father mop a floor or make a salad.

Watch so carefully you will be able to tell a friend exactly how to do the same thing, from start to finish. Look for things you have never paid attention to before—the way a barber spreads out a hank of hair between two fingers and uses them as a guide for the scissors, or the way a moving man with a bookcase on his back staggers a bit before he gets his balance.

Suppose you pick someone who is painting a room. Watch how she pries open the lid of the paint can and stirs the paint with a stick. Watch how she wipes the drips from her brush. How does she stroke the wall—from the bottom or the top? Does she flap the brush back and forth, or does she use one side only? Does she dab at a corner with the tip of the bristles, or does she stroke it with the edge of the brush?

Write down what you have observed in your notebook. Give the painter a name, if you like, and mention everything she does, step by step. Tell how she scratches her nose when her hands are all painty, and how she walks through a wet doorway.

People do useless things, too. They sit around cracking their knuckles or biting their nails. They twist Kleenex into skinny ropes and they ink in the white webs on a black-and-white notebook. They unwind the spiral wire on their memo pad and they braid the fringes on their bathrobe belt. They fidget. How many different fidgets can you count in your classroom in one day? Count your own, too. Let the characters in your stories fidget. Your readers will feel instantly at home with them.

How People Feel   People's behavior changes as their feelings change. When you know someone well, you can usually tell whether he or she is happy or angry or scared. How about when he's embarrassed? Does he, maybe, cover his face? Giggle? Press his lips together? Stare at his toes? What do you do when, say, you walk late into the auditorium and everybody turns around to see who just slammed the door and is clumping down the aisle? What happens to your face? Where do you look? How do you walk?

In a paragraph or two, describe how each of the following people would act. If you tell what happens to these people's hands, feet, mouth, and eyes, it probably won't be necessary to tell how they are feeling.

Laura is sitting in the waiting room, preparing to explain to the principal why she slipped an ice-cream cone down her teacher's umbrella.

Gloria is seized with giggles while performing in the annual chorus recital.

Everybody in Mary Ann's science class has just burst out laughing because she gave a ridiculous response to a question.

Alfred has been sitting in his mother's friend's living room for two hours while the two women discuss the next election.

John Peter shows up for school one day and finds that he's the only one there.

WHAT PEOPLE SAY   Finally, pay attention to what people say. Listen to them. Listen to your friends and to your family. Listen to people on the bus, in the cafeteria line, at the skating rink, in the elevator, and at the movies. Listen when they're happy and when they're angry, when they're excited and when they're bored. Listen to what they say to you and listen to what they say to each other. Eavesdrop.

Dialogue is the spoken conversation in a story, the "he says, she says," part. Dialogue reveals, often better than any kind of description, the moods and personalities of the characters. Like this:

"I came to tell you I'm sorry," said Jim.
"SHUT UP!" Nancy screamed.

Dialogue can also reveal who the characters are, and where. Like this:

"The one thing I hate about these trips," said Amanda, "is the cold. Each year the wind gets sharper and the air gets clammier. And my nose gets runnier. Next year I'm staying home."
"You can't do that," Becky answered. "People expect us to be out on this night."
"Well, there's no reason to travel like *this.* Everybody else flies in airplanes, with cushioned seats and food served on little trays. And movies. Why can't we have movies?"
"Be quiet, Amanda. How can you put a movie screen on a broomstick?" said Becky with a sniff.

And dialogue can tell you what's going on:

"Harold! Please get that parakeet out of my hair!"
"Yes, Mrs. Halloway, I'll try. But I think he has his foot caught in that comb thing on the back of your head."

When you write dialogue of your own, you will often have to let your reader know what the characters already know, and this can be tricky. In the conversation between Amanda and Becky, both characters knew, of course, that they were witches riding on broomsticks, but the reader had to be told. It wouldn't have made sense for them to tell each other who and where they were, so the reader had to catch on through hints and suggestions.

Make up two characters of your own—a girl and her mother, if you like, or a boy and his best friend, a girl and her brother, or a boy and his grandfather. In a few lines of dialogue let them reveal that they are in one of the following places. (Remember, they already know where they are, so they won't say things like, "Well, here we are caught in the laundry chute of the Plaza Hotel!")

> In the dinosaur hall of a museum.
> Locked in the closet of a kidnaper's hideout.
> At a tea party with the Queen.
> In a yo-yo factory.
> In the waiting room of a dentist's office.

Different kinds of people use different kinds of speech. Teachers, babies, kings, ghosts, rock stars, leprechauns, and teenagers all have their own special speech patterns and habits, even though they may all be trying to say the same thing. What's more, a person's speech changes according to the situation. Kids don't usually speak to their teachers the way they speak to each other, and grown-ups don't often speak to each other the way they speak to babies. Try, when you write dialogue, to "get into" your characters, to *be* the person who is doing the talking. If a father is shouting angrily in your story, try to remember all the angry fathers you have ever heard. Then imagine what it would be like to be an angry father yourself.

Make sure, too, that the speech is appropriate to where the people are living and when. A girl of the Civil War period won't use twentieth-century slang, so don't give her lines like "Wow, that guy Abe What's-his-face is, like, far out," even if all the girls you know speak like that.

Read over the following situations and write out a dialogue for each one. Your characters can be angry, apologetic, forgiving, sarcastic, or maddeningly calm. Keep in mind at all times who is speaking and to whom he or she is speaking.

Penny's teacher walks into the classroom unexpectedly the moment Penny decides to perform her Batman act from the top of the teacher's desk.

Jamie is having breakfast at his grandmother's. She has fixed him a bowl of oatmeal, a soft-boiled egg, an English muffin, a glass of orange juice, and a cup of warm milk. Jamie's usual breakfast consists of grape drink and marshmallows.

It is ten minutes before Susan's parents are about to leave for a fancy-dress party. Susan's mother is in the kitchen, pressing her lovely yellow gown. As Susan walks past, she accidentally dumps her bread, jelly side down, on the ironing board, ruining the dress.

Mr. Watkins is at a supermarket checkout counter buying a load of groceries. There are ten impatient people behind him.

It has taken the clerk a long time to ring up and bag everything, and he is growing weary. When he is all through, Mr.
Watkins discovers that he has left his money at home on the
kitchen table.

After you have written your dialogue, recite it back to
yourself out loud and listen. Do the phrases sound real?
Would real people say those things? Do the kids sound
like real kids and not like stuffy grown-ups? Do the
grown-ups sound like real grown-ups and not like make-
believe people reciting lines?

Following are the beginnings of five dialogues. Guess
what the situation and characters might be for each one,
and finish the dialogue accordingly. (Your dialogue will
sound more natural if you avoid a lot of distracting
phrases like "Rudolph chuckled," "moaned Nancy,"
"beamed Uncle John," or "shuddered Mr. Pinn." Usually, "he said," "Joe shouted," or "Mrs. Gregory answered" is enough.)

"Shh, not so loud. They'll hear us."
"Okay, but hold the flashlight steady. I can't see where we're
going."

"What was that noise?"
"I don't know, but it sounds as though somebody is in the
house."

"This is the third time I've had to tell you to stop that
racket!"
"It's not a racket. It's a work of art."

"That is absolutely the wrong thing to wear on an occasion like this."

"This thing? What's the matter with it?"

"You didn't eat that pie that was on the table, did you?"
"Pie? What pie?"

The characters you create for your stories will, of course, develop from your own imagination, but your imagination must first be well stocked with observations of the real people around you. A writer in this respect is a lot like an artist. Before an artist can paint a human figure on canvas, she has to spend a lot of time studying real human figures so she will know exactly where to put the ears and which way the elbows turn. The picture she ends up with may not look like anyone in particular, but viewers will recognize a human being in it and will respond to the kind of human being it seems to be. Writers must know how real people dress and behave and speak before they can dress their make-believe characters, move them around, and put words in their mouths.

The character you end up with will be like a new friend whom you think you just might have met before. Your readers will most likely feel the same way.

8
Plot

You are riding along on your bike with a box containing a fancy cake balanced on the handlebars, when suddenly you skid into a tree. The cake box is on the sidewalk, the bike is on the sidewalk, and you are on the sidewalk, facedown. The worst part is the cake, which you were supposed to take to your aunt and which your mother told you to deliver on foot. You finally struggle to your feet and peer inside the box, where you see what looks like a pink-and-white mud pie. You try to think of something to do, but the only thing that occurs to you is to lean against the tree and cry, which you do. Pretty soon a kid you always thought was a creep comes along and stares at you. You tell him to get lost, but to your surprise, he straightens out your bicycle for you and then begins to inspect the cake. He says that the cake itself is okay; it's just the icing that's ruined. The next thing you know, he's taking you to his house, setting the cake down on the kitchen table, scraping off the icing, making a new icing, spreading it around the cake, and finally taking it with you to your aunt's house. The new cake is not wonderful, but the new friend is, and you end up, in one sense, better off than you were before.

That's a story with a plot.

A plot is the development and outcome of a difficult situation—a problem—in a story. Something happens. Something has to be done about what has happened. Something is done. End of story. Of course, not every problem has a happy solution. You might have ended up with no friend, no bike, no cake, and no allowance for the next month, but that too is an outcome of the problem, unsatisfying as it may seem.

What kinds of problems are worked out in a plot? In real life, men and women struggle against many forces throughout their lives. They struggle against the forces of nature, they struggle against other people, they struggle against themselves. Fiction stories reflect these struggles.

In a struggle against nature, the problem can be the weather: Philip is paddling happily on a lake in a tiny rubber canoe when a violent storm comes up. Or the problem can be an animal: a runaway giraffe chooses Marilyn's house as a refuge and sets up camp in her living room, eating the philodendron by day and sleeping on the Hide-A-Bed by night.

In a struggle against people, the problem can be one person: Joe wants to be captain of the baseball team; so does Patricia. Or it can be a few against many: the city planners want to tear down Jimmy's block and put up a shopping mall in its place.

When characters struggle against themselves, they are

usually fighting something they do or feel that keeps
them from achieving something: Matthew is an over-
eater; Jill breaks into a cold sweat every time she ap-
proaches the edge of a swimming pool; Stanley steals
gumballs from machines.

How is a problem solved? Sometimes by luck or accident: the storm on the lake blows over; the giraffe is
allergic to philodendron and sneezes himself out of the
house; Patricia moves to another city; a fire breaks out on
Jimmy's block and the town planners learn that Jimmy
and his family are more important than a shopping mall.

Sometimes the character solves the problem alone, by
strength or cleverness or persuasion: Philip swims back
to shore; Marilyn coaxes the giraffe out of the house with
a handful of gumdrops; Joe makes a deal with Patricia—
he's captain and she's co-captain for half the year, the
other way around for the rest of the year.

Sometimes there's outside help: Philip's father comes
out in a powerboat and tows Philip home; the kids in
Jimmy's class picket city hall; Jill's gym teacher helps her
into the pool; the whole class gets Matthew to slim down
so he can fit into the Snoopy costume for the school play.

Sometimes there is a change of attitude: Marilyn's family decides that a giraffe is actually a useful thing to keep
around the house; Joe decides he'd rather play cello than
baseball; Stanley decides he'd rather fix gumball machines than break into them.

Or, if the story is a fantasy, then magic can solve the
problem: Supersomebody comes along, plucks Philip
out of the water, and delivers him to his kitchen, where

a bowl of chicken soup awaits him on the table; with her new chemistry set, Marilyn shrinks her giraffe to the size of a toy poodle and keeps him for a pet.

Whatever solution you choose for your problem, it must fit in with the story as a whole. If the story is a realistic one, do not provide a magic solution at the last minute. Give your reader all the clues he needs near the beginning. If Philip saves himself by fashioning a sail out of a paddle and a beach towel, mention these items early in the story. Don't tell your reader in the last paragraph that Philip just happened to have a towel wrapped around his head to keep the mosquitoes out of his hair. That's not fair. If you are writing a magic story in which Philip will sprout wings after swallowing a magic pill, let your readers know early on that they should expect a magic solution.

Remember that even fantasies must make sense. Fairies, witches, goblins, and even giraffes in the living room have only limited abilities. Don't overdo their powers. Readers will accept a giraffe who can handle a Hide-A-Bed, but they may begin to balk if he can slip in and out of the mail slot and disappear in a cloud of steam as well.

Your beginning paragraph is important. In it you will want to let your reader in on a lot of facts—what's happening, where and when it's happening, and to whom it's all happening. You will also want to do something else: make your reader interested enough to continue.

Here are two possible opening paragraphs for the same story. Both provide background information.

I

Once there was a little girl whose name was Victoria. She lived a hundred years ago in a house in the country. One winter she went to visit her grandmother, who lived in the city. It was the first time she'd ever been to the city.

II

The coachman's hand felt cold against Victoria's sleeve as he helped her down to the snowy pavement. She paused next to her small traveling case and squinted down the gaslit street at the rows of stone steps and heavy wooden doors with brass knockers. Never before had she seen houses like these, one up against the other, with no meadows or pastures in between, no rose vines curling at the windows. Which door, she wondered, was her grandmother's?

Which arouses your interest? The first merely states facts, one after another. The second suggests them, so that readers can picture as well as learn what is going on. If your readers can do that, they will probably stay with your story.

Just for practice, write an opening paragraph of your own. You needn't complete the story, although your beginning may be so good you will want to add to it. Look over the following three lists. Pick a character from the PEOPLE column, a locale from the PLACES column, and a kind of day from the WEATHER column. Then choose a time—morning, noon, or night; past, present, or future. These will be the background elements of your story.

PEOPLE	PLACES	WEATHER
Penelope, a girl your age	Secret cave	Sunshine
Hector, a boy your age	Department store	Hurricane
Alexander, a man old enough to be your father	Submarine	Rain
Daphne, a woman old enough to be your mother	Spaceship	Fog
Mrs. Petty, a grandma	Circus train	Snow
Mr. Petty, a grandpa	Gas balloon	Wind
	Abandoned house	
	Rooftop	

Now write an opening paragraph containing all the facts you have chosen, but don't actually state them. Hint at them. Instead of saying that Penelope is a young girl or that Mr. Petty is in a gas balloon, suggest these details by describing their clothing or behavior:

Penelope wore a T-shirt with a picture of a ketchup bottle on the front and her name stamped in green letters on the back.

Mr. Petty looked over the edge of the basket at the town one thousand feet below. Overhead, the huge bubble of blue-and-white nylon swayed in the wind, and he began to sing as he soared out toward the sea.

You can refer to the weather, even if the scene takes place inside an elevator, by mentioning a dripping um-

brella or snowflakes on a collar, wind-tousled hair or
drops of sweat behind the knees.

The style of your story will depend a good deal on who
is supposed to be telling it. A story can be told from the
point of view of one of the characters or from the point
of view of a narrator outside the events. There are several types of viewpoints that writers use, but the three
most common are the *first person*, the *third person*, and the
omniscient.

In the first-person viewpoint, the story is narrated by
one of its characters, and everything that happens is seen
through his or her eyes and spoken through his or her
voice. It sounds like this:

Every time I plan to spend the day loafing around the house,
watching TV, maybe, and eating a ton of Cheez-Doodles, my
mother comes along and nags me to go visit my grandmother.
My grandmother lives at the other end of the woods and visiting her is an absolute drag, but every time she gets sick, which
is practically every other day, my mother thinks I should go
cheer her up. Yesterday was the worst. I had just flopped down
in the big chair with the cushy pillows, to watch the two-thirty
soap, which is my favorite. I had this gigantic bag of Cheez-
Doodles on my lap, and things were really going great on the
show. In two minutes my mother's voice comes in from the
kitchen. "Little Red Riding Hood!" (She always calls me that
because I wear this red riding hood all the time. Actually my
name is Lois.) "Little Red Riding Hood, your poor grandmother is sick today, and I want you to take this basket of cakes
to her."

"Mmmm," I answered, and stuffed another fistful of Cheez-
Doodles into my mouth.

"And be careful not to speak to anyone in the woods." She
always says stuff like that. Little did I know.

In the third-person viewpoint, the events of the story
are also seen through the eyes of one character, but they
are narrated by the author in the author's words. When
other characters are introduced, we see them only as
they appear to our hero or heroine. Like this:

Little Red Riding Hood was picking her way through the
empty soda cans and hot-dog wrappers that littered the path
when she heard a rustling in the surrounding woods. What
crazy fool would want to picnic on a day like this? she wondered, and she shifted the basket of cakes to her other arm.
"Good morning, Little Red Riding Hood," said a voice, and
Little Red Riding Hood spun around. There, among the trees,
stood someone in what was probably last Halloween's wolf
costume. "Where are you going," he asked sweetly, "with that
lovely basket of cakes?"

"I'm going to my grandmother's," she answered, "so get
lost." All she needed, she thought, was some pest in a wolf suit
yakking at her all the way to her grandmother's house.

The word "omniscient" means "all-knowing." In an
omniscient point of view, the narrator knows everything
that is going on at any one time. He or she can take us
into the mind first of one character and then of another,
and tell us what is happening at the same moment in two
separate places. Like this:

Little Red Riding Hood rang her grandmother's bell. If I just drop off the cakes, she thought, and ask her how she's feeling a few times, maybe I can be home in time to catch the three-thirty show. She pressed her finger on the bell again, wondering why it was taking so long for her grandmother to answer.

Inside Grandmother's bed the wolf was hurriedly pulling a lace nightcap over his ears. How come, he wondered, they don't make nightcaps the way they used to? A wolf can freeze his ears off in a thing like this. "Come in, dear!" he called, trying to sound cheerful in spite of an ill-fitting nightcap on his head and a hastily swallowed grandmother in his stomach.

Grandmother searched about for a comfortable position inside the wolf's stomach. It's a bit dark in here, she said to herself, but maybe I can brighten the place up with some nice curtains.

Back in Little Red Riding Hood's living room, Mother switched off the TV and swept the Cheez-Doodle crumbs from the floor. What a nice long visit Little Red Riding Hood is having with her grandmother today, she thought happily. They must be having a lovely chat.

Once you have chosen the viewpoint from which your story is to be told, it is best to stick to it. Remember that each character knows only what she herself feels and sees and thinks. If you have chosen one person through whose eyes everything is seen, don't tell what somebody else sees. The following paragraph is confusing because the person who is telling the story couldn't know what Laura was thinking and feeling:

I slid into the seat next to Laura. This was Laura's first trip on a roller coaster, and she was terrified. Her knees felt weak and her heart was pounding hard. She wondered if she should have come at all.

This is better:

I knew as soon as I sat down next to Laura that she was terrified. Her face turned white as she stared down the track, and I could feel her hand tremble next to mine. "Don't you think we should go back?" she asked.

A writer must decide ahead of time where to begin a story and where to end it. Suppose while Philip is paddling about in his rubber canoe, an explosion of lightning and thunder tears across the lake, throwing him into the water. Chances are that will be the most exciting point of his adventure. It will be your story's *climax*, the moment that will change the direction of the action—Philip will either come out alive or he won't.

How close to the climax should your story begin and end? In some stories the climax comes smack in the middle, with the beginning and the end equally balanced on either side: as much time will be spent telling about Philip's leaving the shore as telling about his reaching it again. In some the climax appears close to the beginning: moments after we find Philip out on the lake, the storm comes up and swamps his canoe. The rest of the story describes how he gets himself out of his fix. In others the climax comes close to the end: Philip has been out on the water a long time watching the storm come up, before he is washed overboard. Not until the last paragraph does he catch sight of a rescuer approaching him in a powerboat.

You are the best judge of how to approach the climax of your story. The important thing to keep in mind is that everything you put in the story must belong in some way to the climax. If it doesn't, better leave it out. You will probably want your readers to be as frightened by the storm as Philip was, so you will take time to show ominous signs of its arrival. Just because a climax takes place only a few moments after the opening of the story, it needn't be reached in just a few words. You may also want your readers to know what Philip was doing out there in the first place, and you will want to devote a line or two to explain that. But forget about his breakfast that morning and the fight he had with his sister.

Take time writing your story. You will probably find that you are more enthusiastic about it at the beginning than when you reach what should be its middle. As a result, your stories may seem top-heavy, with all the careful details and elaborate descriptions occurring near the beginning, while the ending is hurried and abrupt. If you find your enthusiasm running out, leave your story in the middle and come back to it later. Stop at a point when you still have an idea or two left in your head. That way you won't be returning to your page with an empty mind. Another way to avoid producing an overwritten beginning and a hasty ending is to write the middle section first. There's nothing that says you must begin writing your story with its opening sentences. Save them for later, and see if your stories don't come out with better balance.

Sometimes a story becomes unbalanced when too much attention is paid to small details and not enough to important action. Don't use a lot of words getting a character from one place to another or from one day to the next. When you want to move him from here to there or from then to now, don't push him along. Pick him up and plunk him down. Suppose Wendy, a girl in your story, has just discovered that someone tied all her pajamas in a long chain and strung them across her bedroom. She has good reason to speak to her brother about this, and he is down in the kitchen. How do you get her there? The following paragraph has too much detail:

Wendy opened the door of her bedroom and walked across the hall to the stairs. She went down the stairs quickly and raced along the downstairs hall, through the living room and the dining room, until she came to the kitchen, where she found her brother. As soon as she saw him she began to yell at him.

This is better:

In the kitchen, Wendy began to yell at her brother.

In the same way, when you want to move your story forward from one time to another, you must do so in one leap and not minute by minute. Here are some ways to do it:

Five years later Louise was still living on the farm, but many things had changed.

Many times over the next few weeks Harold wondered if he would ever get the chance to escape.

The war went on for twenty years. When it was over, the city was in ruins.

When, five months later, Johanna finally got around to doing her laundry . . .

Later that day Seth discovered his cat, too, was missing.

Suppose you want to go backward in time, to take your readers from now to then. When writers stop the flow of a story in order to provide the reader with a glimpse into the past, they use a device known as a *flashback.* Here are some ways to introduce a flashback:

Joseph wished now that he had never seen Dick the day before, never spoken to him, never accepted his stupid dare.

Maria was pretty fed up with Lucy. Last summer, when they first met, she was glad to have a new friend. Things were different then.

How the school had changed in just five short years!

In many cases it may not be necessary to move your characters around at all in time or place. Your story will hold together if all the action occurs in a small area and within a short period. If a trip isn't necessary, don't take it. If Annette has to buy a new supply of colored chalk for the clubhouse, you don't have to follow her to the

store and back. Just say, "Annette brought back six
boxes of chalk from the store." If Annette's friend Gail
has just had her hair cut to the tops of her ears, tell your
readers how startled everybody was when she walked
into the clubhouse—don't accompany her to the beauty
parlor.

Avoid bringing a lot of characters into your story.
Readers have difficulty keeping track of a lot of people,
so if a character isn't necessary to your plot, leave him
out. If the giraffe in Marilyn's living room causes some
trouble to the woman next door, mention her. Otherwise, don't.

When you are all finished with your story, put it away
for a few days and then come back to reread it. By then
you will have forgotten what you *meant* to say, and you
will discover what you *did* say. Can you follow the plot?
Does it make sense? Can you get into the story right
away or is there too much description in the beginning?
Is the story nicely balanced or is too much attention
paid to details that don't matter very much? The kind
of balance you give your story will often depend on the
type of story it is. In a mystery story you will tell more
about the action than about how people look and dress.
In a magic story you will give more space to how the
magic works than to long conversations among the
characters. In a baseball story you will tell more about
the game than about the scenery. This doesn't mean
you must tell *only* about the game, or the magic, or the

mystery. There is room in every story for descriptions of people and landscapes. You must decide just how much. The more stories you write, the easier it will be for you to make that judgment.

9

Letters

When you sit down to write a letter, chances are it is not because you want to but because you have to.

Maybe you are away from home for a few weeks and your family has insisted that you let them know now and then that you are alive.

Or you have a friend who lives far away, and if you don't answer her last letter, she'll send you another, which will be more than your conscience can handle.

Or you have to thank someone for something, most likely a relative for a gift.

Or you have to ask for something.

There are two kinds of letters, personal and business. A personal letter is the kind you write to a friend or relative or to someone your own age. A business letter is the kind you send to a company or to an adult you don't know. It is often in the form of a request. While there is a standard form for setting each kind of letter on paper, the rules governing business letters are stricter and more formal.

A personal letter can be as creative a piece of writing as a story or a poem. The same skills you have already acquired in transforming observations and perceptions into written prose can be applied to the letter you write to your family when you are away from home. While it is true that your parents would settle for any scrap of paper from you, even if all it said was, "Dear Mom and Dad, I got here okay. Love, Tanya," both you and they would be happier with something that offered some news and was fun to read.

The following letter is a little more informative, but not much, and it isn't much fun to read. Chances are it wasn't much fun to write either.

Dear Mom and Dad,

The kids in my bunk are okay. The scenery is nice. Every day we have arts and crafts. The food stinks. Well, I have to go now.

Love,
Tanya

There are many things that Tanya's letter didn't mention and that her parents would have liked to hear about. In what way are the kids in her bunk "okay"? What's nice about the scenery? What goes on in arts and crafts? What makes the food terrible? Instead of general statements, it is best to give examples. Like this:

Bunk D
Camp Windsong
East Lake, VT 05899
July 3, 19—

Dear Mom and Dad,

Yesterday I got Silly Putty caught in my hair, but Harriet got it out. It took her a whole hour, and she had to miss swimming, but she said she couldn't stand the thought of me with a lump of Silly Putty stuck in my hair for the rest of my life. It wasn't just because it was her Silly Putty. She's really a good friend.

Sometimes, if we get up very early, we can see a mist rising from the lake. It reminds me of a whole bunch of ghosts going for a swim.

I have already made four lanyards in arts and crafts. They are all blue and green, because those are the only colors left. The big kids got to all the pink and silver first.

One thing I miss up here is your cooking. For the past three nights we have had powdered mashed potatoes mixed with water. It tastes like detergent. On Sundays they serve ordinary meals, but they give them fancy names. "Beef Jamboree" is really meat loaf.

Love,
Tanya

The preceding letter is laid out in the standard form for a personal letter. All your personal letters should follow this form. Look it over. Your address goes in the upper right-hand corner. The date appears directly below the address. It is best not to abbreviate anything in either the date or address except the name of a state. Skip a couple of lines and begin your salutation (the "Dear Mom and Dad" part) at the left of the page, about an inch from the edge. In a personal letter a comma follows the salutation. Indent each paragraph. The complimentary close (the "Love" or "Yours truly" part) appears a couple of spaces below the body of your letter and somewhat to the right of the center of the page. It is followed by a comma. Sign your name below the close—first name only to someone you know well, full name to someone who may not be quite certain who you are.

What if there's nothing to say? You can't always be in the middle of a fire at sea or at the deciding game of the World Series when it's time to write a letter. What do you write about when nothing has happened in your life for three straight months? A letter doesn't have to be filled with accounts of exciting events to be newsy. Little things make news too. Getting stung by a bee can, in a well-written letter, become a major occasion:

> 19 Prospect Lane
> Baltimore, MD 21128
> June 15, 19—

Dear Allen,

Yesterday, while I was walking barefoot in the backyard, I suddenly felt an enormous pain under my toe. I thought I had stepped on a sharp rock, but when I looked down I saw a yellow jacket clinging to my foot. The pain was so bad I started screaming like a maniac, and everybody came running out to see what was the matter.

Everybody in my house has a different beesting cure. My mother read somewhere that you're supposed to use meat tenderizer; my father said you're supposed to use baking soda or baking powder, he couldn't remember which; and my brother said that everybody in books uses mud.

Pretty soon they were all arguing with each other. My mother was yelling because my brother was digging up mud from the flower bed, my father was yelling because he said it was ridiculous to put meat tenderizer on toes, and my brother was yelling because no one was letting him dig.

I was just standing there, with my toe swelling up like a fat tomato.

In the end I used all four cures—the mud, the meat tenderizer, the baking soda, and the baking powder. None of them did any good. Here it is twenty-four hours later and my foot still hurts like crazy.

Your friend,
Arthur

What may seem like everyday routines in your life may actually be of considerable interest to someone living far away. The six-foot snowbanks that have been piled at your curbstone for a month will make news to someone who sees nothing but palm trees all winter. They will also make news to someone who has been staring at *ten*-foot snowbanks for a month. Your faraway friends will be happiest with letters that let them compare their lives with yours. Tell them about a project in school, even if it seems ordinary to you. It will either be very similar to something they're doing or totally different. For either reason, they will want to hear about it. Here's an example:

24 Oak Street
Catskill Falls, NY 12872
February 10, 19—

Dear Jenny,

This month our class is doing a project on presidents of the United States. Each person picks the name of a president from a box and then has to *be* that president for a day. I picked Chester Alan Arthur. Nobody ever heard of him except Gary, whose father went to the same college he went to, only not at the same time.

What we do is this: learn all about our president's life and about the history of the country at the time he was president. Then each day a different president takes over the class and pretends that the kids are members of Congress. He tells them about the country's problems, and they're supposed to help decide what to do about them. President Garfield said that his problem was that he was going to be assassinated. I told him to lock himself up in his room that day.

So far I haven't learned anything good about Chester Alan Arthur, except that his wife's name was the same as mine.

Love,
Ellen

A thank-you letter should express two things, gratitude and appreciation. The gratitude part is easy: "Thank you for the dart board." "Many thanks for the musical birdcage." "How kind of you to send me a Ping-Pong table for my dollhouse." The appreciation part is more difficult. It won't do to say "I've always wanted one." Nobody believes that anymore. The uncle who gave you the dart board probably spent time and thought picking it out, and it would make him happy to know that you took notice of whatever special dart-board features led him to make his choice. So before you write your thank-you note, take a good, hard look at whatever it is you are offering thanks for. He would also like to know that you are making use of his gift. If you haven't actually used it yet, tell how you plan to in the future. Here is an acceptable letter:

> 435 Parkway Drive
> West Village, ME 04137
> September 30, 19—

Dear Uncle Sidney,

  Thank you for the dart board you sent for my birthday. What I especially like about it is the way a bell rings every time you hit a bull's-eye. I have hung it on my closet door, and every day after school I practice with it. I haven't actually hit the bull's-eye yet, but I have hit the dart board fourteen times. It is a lucky thing that the darts have rubber tips. My little sister plays too, which is how I know about the bell.

> Sincerely,
> Roland

  A writer of any kind of material—poetry, short stories, essays, or book reports—has to learn what *not* to put in as well as what to include. Nowhere is this more important than in the business letter. Business letters, especially when they are addressed to large organizations, are often read in a hurry. Large organizations get lots of mail. So a business letter, in order to be understood, has to be clear and brief. No extras.

  You will make your business letter easy to read if you

set off each thought in a paragraph of its own. Several paragraphs, one or two sentences long, are easier to grasp than one long paragraph. If you are typing your letter, skip an extra line between paragraphs.

In a letter requesting material, state what you want, why you want it, and how grateful you will be to get it. That's enough. Like this:

> Room 112
> Kingston Elementary School
> Cleveland, OH 44138
> November 13, 19—

Venezuelan Consulate General
7 East 51st Street
New York, NY 10022

Dear Sir or Madam:

My fifth-grade class is studying Venezuela this month, and I am doing a report on Venezuelan education.

Do you have any pictures of Venezuelan schools or universities that I might include in my report? I would especially like pictures of elementary-school classrooms.

Thank you for any help you might offer.

> Yours truly,
> Willie Lee Harrison

The above letter is written in standard business-letter form. It should be a model for every business letter you write. It is slightly different from the personal letter form. Your address and the date appear in the upper right-hand corner, address first, date below. Do not ab-

breviate anything (except the name of the state, if you
wish). Skip a line or two. Write the name and address
of the party you are writing to about one inch from the
left-hand edge of the page. Don't abbreviate anything
here, either. If the person you are writing has an official
title in the organization, put it after a comma following
the name, like this: "Ms. Anna J. Watkins, President."
Skip a line and write the salutation, "Dear Ms. Watkins"—the salutation in a business letter is always followed by a colon (:). If you are writing to an official
whose name you do not know, your salutation should
read "Dear Sir," "Dear Madam," or—if you don't know
whether the official is a man or a woman—"Dear Sir or
Madam." If you are not addressing anyone in particular
in an organization, begin your letter with "Gentlemen." The most popular closing for a business letter is
"Yours truly." It appears two spaces below the body of
the letter, a little to the right of center, and is followed
by a comma. Sign your name directly below the closing.
If you're using a typewriter, type your full name below
your signature.

Take a lot of care in writing a letter of application for a
job. Chances are there will be many other letters inquir-
ing about the same job, and you will want yours to stand
out. First, state what job it is you want and, if possible,
how you heard about it. Then list all the reasons you think
you can handle it well. Mention your experience and your
personal qualifications. It is better to tell why you would

be good for the job than why the job would be good for you. Don't mention the fact that you need the money for a ten-speed bike. Finally, provide information on how you can be reached for an interview.

64 Grandview Terrace
Plainville, MN 55173
June 2, 19—

Box 245
New Village Station
Plainville, MN 55173

Dear Sir or Madam:

I was interested to see your ad for a dog walker in this morning's newspaper, because I think I am just the right person for the job.

I am thirteen years old and have been a dog owner all my life. For the past seven years my family has owned a beagle, and I have been walking it daily since I was eight.

I am known to be reliable by everyone I have worked for. I have delivered newspapers for a year and a half and have never missed a day. In fact, I was the only news-kid to deliver papers during last winter's blizzard.

I have also worked as plant waterer, guinea-pig sitter, parakeet feeder, and baby-carriage pusher for many people in my neighborhood. I am sure they will all tell you that I always perform my job well.

I enjoy being outdoors in all kinds of weather, and I am a good walker. (I made almost $50.00 for my school's walkathon last April by walking fifteen miles *in the rain!*)

I am quite large for my age and should have no trouble handling your four Great Danes.

I hope you will give me a call at 555-5579, so that we can make an appointment for an interview.

> Yours truly,
> Betsy Ann Clarke

Not all letters have to be friendly. Some can be angry. An effective way to express dissatisfaction with the way things are going is to send a letter to someone who has some authority to change them. You *should* send such letters. Receiving complaint mail is often the only way officials find out what the public thinks. The manufacturer of a bubble gum that doesn't bubble should be written to. So should a congressman who is about to vote on an unfair law.

It is possible to express anger without being downright rude. Tell exactly what it is you object to and why. Offer suggestions if you can. No name-calling—your purpose, remember, is to get something changed, not to hurt someone's feelings. Here's a possibility:

> 602 East 83rd Street
> New York, NY 10028
> October 7, 19—

Chew-Chew Chain
Department 3
Elk Mountain City, PA 16739

Gentlemen:

Recently I decided to switch to your brand of bubble gum because I liked its colors. I had never seen plaid bubble gum before. I thought the bubbles would come out plaid too.

The trouble was the bubbles wouldn't come out at all. Each time I tried, the gum would just tear and wrap itself around my tongue in a long string. My friends couldn't get it to bubble either. We tried a whole pack at a time, but that didn't help.

What's more, even if the gum did make bubbles, they wouldn't have been plaid, because the gum turned gray as soon as it was chewed.

I suggest you either improve your product or stop selling it. My friends and I feel cheated.

Yours truly,
Donald Hammerstein

There is one very special bonus to writing letters, even angry ones, that hasn't been mentioned yet, and that is that you usually get letters in reply. Sometimes, the effort is worth it for that alone.

10
Essays and Editorials

Suppose you have no faraway friends, you haven't received any birthday presents recently, you're not away at camp or boarding school, and you haven't chewed any defective bubble gum in a while. You have no one to send a letter *to*. Then maybe you would like to write an *essay*. An essay is like a letter to no one in particular. It expresses your feelings, thoughts, ideas, or opinions on a subject—any subject. It is often about ordinary things.

You have doubtless written many essays already, without necessarily calling them that. The compositions you turned in on how you spent your summer or why the cat is your favorite pet were all essays. So were the written opinions you composed for the class or school newspaper.

An essay doesn't have to be in the form of a report on an assigned topic. An essay can, instead, be a means of putting into written words those shadowy fragments of ideas that slip in and out of your mind all day without announcing that they are there. Unlike other forms of prose, an essay needn't have a recognizable beginning, middle, and end. Often it is written much the way you think, in a stream of loosely connected scraps, where one idea leads to another.

How? Pick up some object or other and stare at it for a while. Suppose it's a rubber ball. Give it a bounce or two. Roll it around between your hands. Rub it on your cheek. Sniff it. Spit on it and wipe it clean. One of these actions is going to make you think of some similar experience. Let your mind wander. Maybe you will be reminded of having your own face rubbed clean. Maybe that will remind you of visiting your relatives. Maybe that will remind you of the time you put your foot through the porch door at your aunt's house. Maybe you will want to write about just that experience. You might begin it like this:

I was polishing the surface of a rubber ball the other day, watching it get pinker and pinker, smoother and smoother. My mother used to clean my face in exactly that way, wetting her handkerchief with her tongue and rubbing it against my cheek until I thought she would wear it down to my jawbone. She always cleaned my face this way just before we arrived at my aunt's house every Sunday afternoon. Sometimes I enjoyed these visits and sometimes I didn't. Once, it was a disaster.

Notice how in the following essay the sight of a television antenna brought on a chain of loosely related thoughts, some of them going back many years to the author's childhood.

Of all the objects in the treeless city block outside my window, the television antenna on the roof across the street offers me my only clue to the presence of the wind. Frail and graceful as a flower growing from some tiny fertile crack in a meadow of tar, it quivers on its shallow-rooted stem at every wayward gust.

I am not quite correct; it does not quiver alone, for it has a shadow.

Antenna and shadow together tremble and shiver each time their common nerve is struck, which at this time of year is often. But how different their responses! The antenna, erect and proud, confines itself to modest twists and turns, like a child shuddering in the cold. The shadow is a baser thing. Writhing and sprawling across the tar, it is like some lazy, beached creature of the sea, giving itself up to the warmth of the late-afternoon sun.

With every shift in wind the shadow changes shape. At times it is a window, vast and barred, admitting neither light nor hand, and then, all at once, it is a tic-tac-toe, devoid of X and O and stenciled by some drunken pen. Next it is a clothesline tangled on the rooftop floor, its linen cargo long since blown away.

Years ago my Uncle Will would turn out all the lights but one and with his hands cast a parade of shapes across our living-room wall. Like the shadow on the roof across the street, they would shift in the blink of an eye from one figure to another: a rabbit, first, with folded ears and twittering nose; a peacock next, with a five-feathered tail; and then, the one I dreaded most, a wolf with snapping jaws and one tiny, miraculous, terrifying eye that would send me screaming from the room.

How did he manage that eye? Many times since, using the same wall and the same lamp—for I live now where I lived then—I have tried to reproduce that wolf, and though I manage well with ear and jaw, I cannot get that perfect point of light, that single eye that sought me out in every corner of the room and pierced me to the bone.

To this day I cannot look at any shadow, whether it be that caricature of myself stretching from my feet on the afternoon pavement, the heavy gray shroud cast by a skyscraper over half the city, the rare black arc that creeps now and again across the face of the moon, or the giant tic-tac-toe on the roof across the street—I cannot look at any shadow without searching nervously for that tiny circle of light, that cold, sharp eye, that tells me I am being watched.

An essay doesn't have to explain or prove anything. It can simply *reveal*. Often it is a kind of whispered secret. Not the kind you promised your best friend never to repeat. The kind, instead, that tells what you are really like inside. The kind you'd probably think too silly to expose.

Such as what? Things you like and things you hate, for instance. Do you secretly like some things that everybody else seems to hate? Head colds, maybe, or turnips or piano lessons? Or do you secretly hate some things that everybody else seems to enjoy, like zoos, dodgeball, Halloween, or staying up late? How about an essay on things you secretly like or secretly hate?

Or how about secret, pointless pastimes? Do you count things? Do you count all the stairs to your friend's apartment, all the paving blocks on your street, all the pickets on the fence around your school, all the stories in a building? Are you an alphabet checker? Do you check to see how many letters of the alphabet appear on cereal boxes and candy wrappers? Do you make little words out of big words? Are you a number adder? Do you add up numbers on license plates and doorways? Are you an alphabetizer? Do you arrange all the names of your classmates in alphabetical order? An essay on pointless pastimes just might create a spark of recognition among all those readers who are thing counters and alphabet checkers themselves.

You can write a how-to essay. Not the useful, factual kind on how to grow an avocado or bake brownies, but a set of instructions for eating spaghetti, for instance, or suppressing a sneeze, or putting on a wet bathing suit, or answering the phone with bread dough on your hands. Or you can write about all these things in an essay entitled "How to Perform Seemingly Impossible Tasks Gracefully."

Imagine a pen pal living halfway around the world. He or she has never been to your country and is unfamiliar with the way you dress, what you eat, how your school is run, the games you play. Everything you do, in fact, is a matter of great interest. How about writing a letter to such an imaginary person, describing one ordinary thing you did yesterday?

Skateboarding would be an amazing activity to someone who had never laid eyes on a skateboard. Describe what the skateboard looks like and how it works. Tell about how you steer it by shifting your body from side to side, and how you make it mount curbs. Tell about how it feels to coast downhill, with the breeze blowing your hair back and your pant legs flapping like a flag. Tell what the scenery looks like as it streaks by the corners of your eyes, and tell how scared you get when you think you're going to hit a parked car. This will not be a letter to mail, of course, but one to keep for yourself, for it will end up being an essay.

An essay doesn't have to be about yourself. It can be about your surroundings. People you know are part of your surroundings, and an essay can be about them. Dogs you know are also a part of your surroundings, and so are cats. Avoid saying that your cat is cute and fluffy and that he has a long tail. Most cats are cute and fluffy and have long tails. Tell instead how he once got his tail caught in the cactus and dragged it across the living-room rug, or how you once made your bed while he was inside it and you didn't find out until three hours later.

The tree in your backyard is part of your surroundings, and so is the ladybug that crawls up its trunk. The street on which you live is part of your surroundings, and so is the backhoe that is digging it up. Everything that is part of your surroundings in some way involves you, even if all you do is glance at it for a second. And anything that involves you can set your mind off in a chain of ideas which, when put into writing, becomes an essay. A fight between two bunches of kids in the school yard may get you thinking about injustice and cruelty and war. You might want to put your ideas in an essay, beginning with a description of the fight and ending with the opinion that if kids learned how to settle arguments without bloodying each other's noses, there might be fewer wars when they grew up.

Such an opinion essay might appear in a school publication in the form of an *editorial.* An editorial is an essay that expresses the opinion of the editors of a newspaper or magazine. It can be on any subject whatever, although it is usually related to matters covered by the newspaper itself. If you are not one of the editors, you may submit a *guest editorial*, which will appear with your name. Other editorials, because they speak for the publication rather than for any individual, are unsigned.

An editorial should accomplish two things—express an opinion and persuade others to agree with it.

Not that you will succeed in winning everyone over to your side. No argument can do that. You can only persuade, and you will persuade best if your tone is reasonable and your writing is clear. Even if you are angry enough about something to smash dishes over it, keep a quiet voice. Excitable writing does not convince. Neither does confused writing. Your editorial will be successful if it is quiet and if it is understandable. In this sense it is like a business letter. Short sentences are better than long ones. Familiar words are better than strange ones.

Even when an editorial appears in a class newspaper whose readers already know about the school yard fight that is its subject and may even have participated in it, it is good policy to assume that no one is familiar with the facts. People want to read details of an event they have already witnessed. The experience then becomes more real. So, instead of merely referring to "that fight that took place in the playground yesterday," begin your editorial with background information. Like this:

A fight broke out on the playground yesterday because of a torn jacket. Some members of Miss Goldstein's class took José's goose-down jacket without his permission and used it for second base. When Dolores scored a double, the jacket tore and most of its feathers spilled out.

At first there was just a lot of arguing. Pretty soon, though, kids started hitting and punching one another. By the time the fight was over, two kids were injured, David with a bent finger and Alison with a bloody nose. Agnes had to be sent home because she has asthma and is allergic to feathers.

Readers will be more inclined to share your point of view if you explain not only what you feel but why you feel it. Instead of "It's bad to fight," tell why you think so. Back your opinion up with facts:

When a fight breaks out, nobody gains. José still has no jacket, Dolores's double was never counted, a lot of kids who used to be friends are now enemies, and the whole class has been punished by having to give up a week of recess.

Your thoughts on the playground fight, though, did not stop here. Your mind was set wandering into territories as distant as international conflicts and wars, and it was these wanderings that caused you to write your editorial in the first place. In your conclusion, you will refer to all these broader issues. (Because an editorial is supposed to represent the opinions of all the editors—even if there is only one—the first-person *plural* pronoun is always used when you refer to yourself. Say "we" instead of "I" and "us" instead of "me.")

We think that the damage of a fight like this is greater than a torn coat or a week spent indoors. Lots of times countries go to war with each other because their leaders don't know how to settle arguments peacefully. Ten years from now the people in this class will be grown up. If they don't learn now how to settle disagreements without hitting each other over the head, what will they be like when they are old enough to use guns and drop bombs?

Every thought in your head can be the opening of an essay. Choose one and follow it wherever it goes. Follow it as you would follow a rabbit through the woods, down one path and up another, through spins and turns, backtracks and dead ends. Don't worry where it takes you. The farther it goes, the greater the adventure.

11
School Reports

You may not think of a science or a social-studies report as "creative" writing. Creative writing seems to deal mostly with things that you make up out of your own head, not with facts that you must find in books and encyclopedias. Actually, any writing, fact or fiction, is creative if it reflects the personal perceptions or thinking of the author and is expressed in his or her own words. Your report on frogs or zeppelins can be creative if the planning, organization, and writing are your very own.

Of course, the *facts* won't be your very own. You must look those up in books and other sources, and you must present them accurately. But the *choice* of facts will be yours, and so will the order in which they appear and the words in which you explain them.

Writing a report is a matter of making decisions. What should the report be about? What information should be covered? What books should be used? How should the report be organized? What should be left out?

Of all the decisions you are required to make, the easiest will probably be the first one, "What should the report be about?" Usually the topic is assigned to you, and if it isn't, your choice will probably be limited to a certain area.

Your next decision, "What information should be covered?" will be harder, and your choices will be made not all at once, but little by little, as your report progresses. Suppose your topic is frogs. You may have some questions yourself you'd like to have answered on the subject of frogs before you even begin. What do frogs eat? Where do they live? Can you find them all over the world? What kinds are there? Do they bite? How long do they live? What's the difference between a frog and a toad? Do they come in different colors? Is it true they give you warts?

Write all these questions down. Not one after another in a list, but with lots of space in between or on separate pieces of paper. As you do your research, you will find the answers to some questions and not to others. Still others will seem unimportant and you will decide to drop them. And other, new questions will arise all the time. If your subject is one you have barely heard about, your only beginning question may be "What is it?" and then all your questions will occur to you after you have started your research.

Where should you look for the facts you need? Encyclopedias, books, pamphlets, and magazine articles are the most frequently used sources of information for reports. They can serve different purposes. An encyclopedia is a good place to begin. In a few paragraphs or, at most, a few pages, an encyclopedia can provide material on all the important areas of your subject: where frogs live, what they eat, how they mate, how they develop from tadpoles, how they vary, how the different parts of their bodies function, and when they first appeared on earth. What an encyclopedia does not do is provide information in great detail. It may list a few common species of frogs, but it won't have room to describe all their characteristics. And if your report is on only one aspect of frogs—how African frogs adapt to their environment, for instance—an encyclopedia may be altogether inadequate.

So you will want to look at some frog books too. A book can deal fully with topics that an encyclopedia can mention only briefly. A book can take its time. Rather than simply list different species of frogs, a book can describe many in detail, explaining their habits and characteristics and showing you how to tell them apart. A book can take the time to describe rare forms of frog life, and you might learn about the tiny poisonous creatures from South America and the fierce leaf frogs of Southeast Asia that eat each other up.

It isn't always necessary to read an entire book to get the material you need. If you have some idea of what areas you are going to cover, you can select from the table of contents or the index just those pages that contain what you want. In this way you can gather information from several books rather than just one.

Magazine articles and pamphlets often contain material that doesn't appear in books, and it is a good idea to look at these too. They are, of course, shorter than books, but often they deal with only one aspect of the subject—tree-dwelling frogs in North America, maybe—and they go into it in great detail. Libraries have current and back issues of dozens of magazines on hand. A guidebook—a good one is *Readers' Guide to Periodical Literature*—helps you find articles on the subject you are interested in. Your librarian will show you how to use it. He or she will also help you locate pamphlets on your subject.

How do you put it all together? Organizing a report is not easy. The number of facts you find will seem more than you know what to do with. Some may answer questions you have already written out, others may answer questions you never thought to ask. There may be a whole section in a book on how long it takes for a frog to shed its skin, when you didn't know that a frog shed its skin at all. Some facts seem to belong together, and others don't seem to belong with anything. What comes first? What do you put next?

As you read, you will be taking notes. It is almost impossible to remember all the important facts you read without writing them down as you go along. Note taking is not the same as copying. When you come across a fact you want to remember, close the book for a moment and write it down in as few words as possible. If it answers a question you have already prepared, write it in the space you have provided. If not, put it under a new question. Here is a paragraph on frogs from *The World Book Encyclopedia.* Read it over and then look at the notes that were taken from it.

The first frogs appeared on earth about 180 million years ago. About 2,700 species of frogs and toads have developed from these early ancestors. Some species spend their entire life in or near water. Others live mainly on land and come to the water only to mate. Still other species never enter the water, not even to mate. Many kinds are climbers that dwell in trees. Others are burrowers that live underground.

NOTES

180,000,000 years old.
2,700 species of frogs and toads.
Some live mostly in water.
Some live mostly on land but mate in water.
Some only on land.
Some climb trees, others burrow underground.

Put all the notes on a frog's habitat—that is, where it lives—under your question "Where do they live?" The note about the 2,700 species will be included in the question "What kinds are there?" The note about how many years frogs have existed on earth belongs under a new question, "How long have they been around?" because you hadn't thought about that before you began.

Then what? What do you do with your questions once they are answered? You will find as you go along that the books and encyclopedias you use divide your subject into separate sections. The answers to your questions "Do frogs bite?" and "What do they eat?" might both be found in a section headed "Parts of the Body," where you will learn about the structure of a frog's mouth and how its tongue is used to catch insects. You may also discover that the two questions "What kinds are there?" and "Do they come in different colors?" are really the same and belong in a section labeled "Species."

The more reports you do, in fact, the more you will recognize familiar subject headings. All animal subjects will probably cover material that can be divided into the following categories:

EVOLUTION.   What were its prehistoric ancestors?

CLASSIFICATION.   To what division of the animal kingdom does it belong? Is it an insect, a fish, a reptile, an amphibian?

HABITAT.   What are its natural surroundings? Does it live in the desert, in the mud, or in caves? In hot places or cold? On every continent or on only one or two?

PARTS OF THE BODY.   What are its physical characteristics? Has it a trunk, red feathers, a tail, webbed feet, fangs? How do the parts of its body function? How do they help it to adapt to its habitat?

HABITS.   How does it behave? Does it sleep in a tree? Does it hunt at night?

DEVELOPMENT.   How does the animal change and grow throughout its life?

REPRODUCTION.   How does it mate? Are the babies hatched from eggs or are they born live?

SPECIES.   What varieties of the animal are there?

RELATIONSHIP TO PEOPLE AND OTHER ANIMALS.   How is the animal useful to mankind? What are its dangers to people? What animals does it threaten? What are its natural enemies? How is it endangered by people?

The answer to your question "What's the difference between a frog and a toad?" might go in the "Classification" section. Information on "How long do they live?" belongs under "Development." The warts question, if you have found the answer to it, might be put under "Relationship to People and Other Animals."

You don't have to include all these categories in your report, and you may add some that aren't here. You may do a report on only one section, but you will probably find that you will use material from other sections just the same. A report on the development of the frog from tadpole to adult will include information on parts of the body, where it lives, and how it reproduces.

Not all reports, of course, are about animals. Some are about famous people, some are about wars, some are about countries, some are about machines. All subjects, though, can be divided into sections. A famous woman's life can be divided according to years: early childhood, school days, early adulthood, maturity, old age. A report on a country can be organized according to geographic areas: north and south, highlands and lowlands. Or it can be divided into characteristics: customs, climate, natural resources, and industry. You can report on a machine by explaining its stages of development, ancient to modern.

What do you put first? When you are organizing a report chronologically, or according to a sequence of time, you naturally start with the early stages of your subject: the early years of someone's life, the events leading up to a war, the beginning days of an animal's life, or the early forms of a machine. When your report is organized according to separate topics, begin with the big general ones: tell about how all frogs are amphibians before you tell about the insects they eat. Tell where a country is located before you tell what kind of clothing its people wear. Tell what a machine is used for before you tell how its gears work.

What do you leave out? The information you collect from your books and encyclopedias will probably be more than you can include in your report. You might learn, for instance, that some of your facts apply only to toads, which are different from frogs, and you may decide not to use those notes at all. Or you may choose, once you get started, to limit your report to only two topics, "Habitat" and "Parts of the Body." Where will you put what you learned about warts? Nowhere. Leave it out. Some facts do very nicely just being carried around in your head, and the nonconnection of frogs to warts may be one of them.

By now you will have your report carefully arranged, with the answers to your questions placed neatly in proper sections. All you have left to do is write it.

By far the most troublesome aspect of writing a report

is getting it in *your* words and not your source's. When you read a fact in the encyclopedia, you may not be able to think of any other way of saying it yourself. "The first frogs appeared on earth about 180 million years ago" seems like the only possible wording for that information. How can you do any better? You will probably find yourself substituting a word here and there and rearranging another, like this: "Frogs first showed up on this planet around 180 million years ago." But that's not your own writing; it's someone else's, made over.

The problem is that the fact becomes all tied up in your mind with the words that tell it. That is why it is important to write from notes and not from the book. By the time you refer to the note "180,000,000 years old," which you took down when you were just collecting information, you will have forgotten what the encyclopedia said, and you will be able to express your fact in any words of your choosing. You might write something like this: "Frogs have been around for a long time—about 180 million years."

When you have reached this point, though, you will have many other notes on the age of frog life on earth, so that that one detail may become part of a longer paragraph:

The great dinosaurs *Tyrannosaurus rex* and *Triceratops* were roaming the earth when frogs as we know them today first appeared. That was 180 million years ago. The frog was probably descended from the *Eryops*, which was an early amphibian that grew to be five or six feet long.

Always include specific facts wherever you can. It is better to say "Some frogs grow to thirteen inches in length" than "Some frogs get to be very big." Remember, too, to vary your sentences. Don't begin them all with "The frog . . ."; let some sentences be long, others short.

While most of your report will be your original work, there may be occasions when you will want to include some short selections exactly as they appear in a book. This is not copying—it is quoting. You must, however, put quotation marks around all such material, and you must tell where the quotation is from.

It is important, in fact, to list all the sources you used in gathering your information, whether you quoted directly from them or not. Such a list is called a *bibliography*, and it should appear at the end of every report. To list a book in a bibliography, begin with the name of the author, last name first, and follow it with a period. Next comes the name of the book. Capitalize the beginning letter of each important word, underline the whole title, and end it with a period. The remaining information can be found on the front and back of the book's title page: the city where the book was published, followed by a colon (:); the name of the publisher, followed by a comma; the date of publication, followed by a period. It will all look like this:

Schoenknecht, Charles A. <u>Frogs and Toads.</u> Chicago: Follett Publishing Company, 1960.

Keep your report when your teacher has returned it to you. The nice thing about a report is that it becomes a source of information itself. Months later, when you're doing a watercolor of a lily pond in art class and you can't remember how many toes to put on the frog's hind leg, you'll know just where to go to look that up.

12

Book Reports

Book reports help everyone. They help you, the reviewer; and they help your classmates, the readers. You benefit because writing about a book makes you think about it more carefully and get more meaning from it. Your classmates benefit because they learn about a book they might otherwise never have heard of.

Your obligation as a book reviewer is to tell your readers two things: what the book is about and what you thought of it.

Telling what a book is about involves more than relating its story or listing its facts. Readers want to know more than that. They want to know what a book is *like.* Is it funny, sad, or scary? Does it have lots of description, lots of dialogue, lots of suspense, or lots of jokes? Is it mostly adventure, mostly family life, or mostly fantasy? Is it fiction, nonfiction, or a little of each? Does it list lots of facts one after the other, or does it sprinkle them around here and there so that you don't realize you're learning something?

It is a good idea when you write about a book to ask

yourself what the author may have wanted you to get out of it. Maybe he simply wanted to write a good, scary mystery that would turn you pale, or a wacky fantasy that would make you giggle. Maybe she wanted you to learn about life on an Israeli kibbutz or an American prairie. Maybe he wanted you to think a little about the problems of drugs, divorce, or death.

Knowing what the author hoped to accomplish in a book will help you decide what to say about it. A novel whose purpose is to portray life on an Israeli kibbutz may not have much plot, so you will concentrate on kibbutz living in your report and not attempt to tell a story. A mystery, on the other hand, is mostly plot, so you won't spend much time with the characters or their surroundings. And you will deal mostly with people and their problems in a report on a book about a boy with an alcoholic brother.

It is not wise to begin your report with "This book is about . . .": first of all, readers may be tired of such openings, and second, the only way to complete such a line is to sum up the whole book, which is difficult to do all at once. Instead, start right in with a direct account of what is going on in the book. If you are reviewing a mystery, relate the first major event. Remember that you are *writing* and not *telling* about what happened. Use a writer's words. Don't write "this" when you mean "a." You may *say*, "This girl lives with her mother in this crazy-looking house," but you *write*, "*Nancy* lives with her mother in *a* crazy-looking house." Use the present tense, as though everything were happening right now. Like this:

Stephanie senses something is wrong the minute she steps into her father's Laundromat. Although the door has been tightly locked all night, one of the driers is turned on, and a full load of wash is tumbling around behind its window. When Stephanie turns off the motor, she discovers a strange assortment of clothing—pants, dresses, and children's suits—all dating from the eighteenth century!

If the author's purpose in writing the book was to give an account of family life in special surroundings, then start off with a description of the setting. Again, use the present tense:

Jaap and his family have recently arrived in New Amsterdam from Holland. Their life would seem strange to us today. Their house has a thatched roof and a tile oven. Jaap sleeps in a bed built into the wall. Each night he warms the mattress by rubbing it with a brass pan filled with hot coals. The family throws its garbage out on the streets, where it is eaten up by pigs.

Be specific in this opening section of your book report. Give examples. Your readers won't learn much if you just write, "The Grubbs like animals a lot and do many unusual things with them." What kinds of things? Describe a couple, perhaps like this:

The Grubb family lives in a New York City apartment house with so many animals they don't know which way to turn. Mr. Grubb keeps his lizard collection in the bathtub. Whenever anyone wants to take a bath, he has to scoop up all the lizards in a shower cap and put them in a clothes hamper. Mrs. Grubb has a pigeon who sits in the bread drawer all day, wearing a tiny bonnet. A family of mice lives in a handkerchief box. Each afternoon Mrs. Grubb ties the box, with all the mice, onto a roller skate, and wheels them up and down the the street for an airing.

If you are reviewing a biography or history, your report will be written in the past tense, because you will be dealing with real events that have already taken place:

When Jackie Robinson was a high-school student in Pasadena, California, he was a star athlete in baseball, football, basketball, and track. Later he became the first athlete at UCLA to win a letter in all four sports.

It isn't necessary to tell about the entire book in such careful detail. You don't want to reveal too much about the book's contents, anyway. If you give the story away, you spoil it not only for future readers, who want to come upon its surprises themselves, but for the author as well, who wants a chance to tell it in his or her own way. So after you have established the background, sum up the rest of the book more generally, without revealing any important secrets.

Little by little, Stephanie learns the secret of the mystery family that has come out of the past and washes its clothes in her father's Laundromat.

Jaap's life is sometimes fun and sometimes unhappy. He likes to help his family by making candles, baking bread, and even carrying water in buckets on a yoke. But there are hard times too. His family gets sick often, and once their house catches fire.

The Grubbs invite more and more animals into their apartment until finally they invite one too many.

Your enjoyment of a book depends as much on its *style*—that is, the way it is written—as on what it is written about. Every author has his or her writing style. You have a writing style of your own. Sometimes you can guess who the author is just by a book's style. Some authors use lots of description in their books, and others use lots of dialogue. In some books the sentences are short and quick; in others they are long and complicated, sometimes taking up a whole paragraph. Some books are written in the slangy language of a ten-year-old, and others are written in elegant prose. The style of a book written today will be different from the style of a book written a hundred years ago. These are the things you automatically check out when you riffle the pages of a new book, making up your mind whether to read it. They are the things your readers want to learn about too. Tell them, also, about any unusual *form* your book might follow—is it a diary? a series of letters? the reminiscence of an old man? You might discuss the style and form of a book like this:

The Story of Jaap was written in 1919, and the style sounds old-fashioned today. The author seems to be talking to very small children, although the words she uses are sometimes difficult. Every once in a while she asks questions like "Wasn't that thoughtful of Jaap?" There is a lot of dialogue, but it is hard to believe that children ever talked like that. Everybody sounds very goody-goody. There are twelve chapters in the book, and each one tells about a different month in the year.

End your report by giving your opinion of the book. What did you think of it? Don't just label it "interesting" or "boring"; give your reasons for liking or disliking it. Or, for that matter, liking *and* disliking it; sometimes you have mixed feelings about what you read. You may have liked your book because it was an animal story and you like all animal stories, but try to find a reason why other people might like it too. How about the characters? Did they remind you of yourself? Did you get mad and happy and sad along with them? Did you keep wishing that you had been part of the story? Was the plot full of surprises? Did you feel at home with the atmosphere? Say so. Here's what you might say about a book you liked:

All the Grubbs is a special kind of animal story. Although the adventures with the animals are always funny and full of surprises, what makes the book so wonderful is getting to know the Grubb family. They are the kind of people you wish were your next-door neighbors.

With a book that you liked a little and disliked a little, tell about both feelings:

What I liked about *Jackie Robinson, Star Athlete* was the way it described the action in certain baseball games. I really felt as though I were right there in the stands, watching every move. What I didn't much like was that everyone in the book sounded phony, and I never felt that I got to know what Jackie Robinson was really like.

There is no reason to say you liked a book when you didn't. It may have been too easy for you or too hard; too long, too wordy, too silly, too sad. Tell why you didn't like it. Here's one way:

While *The Haunted Laundromat* is exciting and scary in parts, I found it unbelievable. Stephanie Lark is too perfect. She's too smart, too well-dressed, too polite, too good, and too lucky. No eleven-year-old is like that. Another trouble with the book is that I guessed the ending when I was only halfway through.

You will probably end up writing more favorable opinions than unfavorable ones, because you will most likely finish the books you like and put aside the ones you can't stand. And it is best to report only on those books you have read all the way through.

POETRY

13

What Is Poetry?

Every now and then you may feel so terrific or so angry or so sad or so dreamy that you have to stop everything you are doing and just *feel*. Sometimes the feeling becomes so wonderful, even if it is an unhappy one, that you wish somehow you might save it, seal it in a special box, maybe, or preserve it in a jar, so you could have it whenever you wanted it. Or sometimes you may notice something that is beautiful or ugly or scary or funny or gruesome, and you may wish you could seal that, too, in a box or jar, to keep forever.

Because you are a writer, though, you don't need a magic container to keep wonderful moments in. You can save what you feel and what you see in written words. Not just ordinary words either. When something very special happens to you, you will want to preserve it in words that are just as special.

When you have put in writing some of these impressions, using words that you have chosen with care, very likely you will find to your surprise that you have composed a poem, because that, more or less, is what a poem is: a feeling or a happening put into very special words.

Of course, there are many definitions of poetry, and everyone arrives at one that suits him best, but this will do until you can make up one of your own.

What kind of feelings? Anger, for one. All kinds of anger: anger over war and pollution or anger over stubbing your toe on the refrigerator door. And joy, for another. Joy over winning a battle or joy over feeling a snowflake sting your tongue. Loneliness. Sorrow. Love and hate. And terror: the terror of an earthquake or the terror of facing an audience when you're the star of a play.

What kind of happenings? A happening can be a lengthy event—a battle of long ago, a courtship, or a visit—from Paul Revere, maybe, or from Saint Nick. A happening can be a tiny moment—the sight of a gnat imprisoned in a raindrop or the sound of a goose crying in the sky. Or it can be something that never quite happens at all—it can be a happening of the mind, a moment of wondering. What is it like to be a snail, a ghost, a speck of dandelion fluff? Suppose tears were made of ginger ale, and where do witches sleep?

What makes words "special"? In some poems, words are special because they rhyme with each other or in some way sound alike. Sometimes words are special because they have a musical beat. They have either a rhythm that can be clapped out, as in a song, or just a vague swing that makes your voice go up and down when you speak them. Some words are special because they have a pleasing sound when spoken all together. Even if you don't know their meaning, they *sound* good—they sing or roar or bang or whisper. Sometimes words are special because there are so few of them. One word in a poem might say as much as half a dozen in a school composition.

But words don't have to sound alike to belong in a poem, nor do they have to possess a musical beat, although much of the poetry we are familiar with has both rhyme and rhythm. Lines of poetry don't have to begin with capital letters or be grouped into regular stanzas either, although poetry is often more recognizable when it is arranged that way. Mostly, words in a poem are special because when you read them, you want to hold on to each one. Each one is necessary. If you let one go, it would be like removing a glass pane from a stained glass window. Each is the only one you could possibly use.

Now read the following poem aloud. When you are finished, read the paragraph that comes after it. Both express the same idea, but the first is written in the language of poetry, although it doesn't rhyme or have a fixed form, and the second is written in the language of prose. How can you tell the difference?

A Warm Winter Day

The mist condenses.
The foliage drips
And drips

High in the tree
Next to the Chinese pine
Two peacocks sit;
Their tail feathers hanging
Bedraggled

The fountain is unfreezing.
Below the cracked ice-lumps
Goldfish wait.

Seed pods wait
With their sealed orders.

JULIAN COOPER

And now, the same idea expressed in prose:

There is water dripping constantly from the leaves. Two
peacocks with long, ragged tail feathers are sitting in the tree
next to the Chinese pine tree. There are some goldfish under
the melting ice of the fountain, waiting for winter to be over.
Some seed pods are also waiting for the end of winter, when
they will sprout into their own particular plants.

A poem is your personal response to your personal
world—the world you see and hear and touch with your
fingertips, and the world inside your mind. A poem can
be serious or it can be fun. It can be a cry or it can be
a giggle. It is written in words that you alone choose, one
by one, because you alone know that they belong. A
poem, like a dream, belongs only to you.

14

Feelings

Lonely, Mad . . . Frightened, Glad

A poem can be about anything at all. It can be about watermelons or T-shirts or thunderstorms. Or it can be about something that cannot be seen or heard, something deep inside you—a wish, a fear, a dream; love, hate, anger. It can be about your feelings.

A feeling inside your body seems harder to describe than an object in your hand. It has no shape, no color, no sound. It doesn't move. But a feeling, like an object, makes you stop and take notice.

Feelings make you want to do something—to kiss a friend, tear up your room, hug yourself, run away—and you can write a poem about just that.

Feelings make you want to change things—pull them down or build them up—and you can write a poem about that.

Feelings make you think you're something else—a lonely gull, an angry wind, a frightened mouse, a kite leap-frogging over the trees—and you can write about that.

Next time something makes you angry, take notice, if you can, of what happens to your body—how your lips tighten, your teeth clench, your breathing deepens, your heart beats, your face pounds. What do you wish you could do when you are angry? Suppose your house had an "angry room" where you could do anything you liked—slam doors, break chairs, scream, kick holes in windows. Anything. What would you do? What angry colors would you splash on the walls and what angry noises would you shout to the ceiling?

Maybe, instead of being the human being that you are, you would like, now and then, to turn into something more ferocious. A bear is a convenient thing to be when you are having a tantrum, and so is a hurricane or a witch or a tidal wave. Here is what one nine-year-old would do if she could be a cat whenever she got angry:

Anger

When I'm mad,
I wish I were a cat,
So I could stretch out my claws
and scratch everybody.
I would use my loudest,
fiercest,
most ear-piercing screech.
I would jump
all over people,
and ruin things,
as though
there were no end,
and I'd flash my eyes
their brightest
and scariest.

ANNA LAW

And here is a hate poem by someone who thought it might be handy to turn his tongue into a quiver full of darts:

I Wish My Tongue Were a Quiver

I wish my tongue were a quiver the size of a huge cask
Packed and crammed with long black venomous rankling
    darts.
I'd fling you more full of them, and joy in the task,
Than ever Sebastian was, or Caesar, with thirty-three
    swords in the heart.

I'd make a porcupine out of you, or a pin-cushion, say:
The shafts should stand so thick you'd look like a
    headless hen
Hung up by the heels, with the long bare red neck
    stretching, curving, and dripping away
From the soiled floppy ball of ruffled feathers standing on
    end.

You should bristle like those cylindrical brushes they use
    to scrub out bottles,
Not even to reach the kindly earth with the soles of your
    prickled feet.
And I would stand by and watch you wriggle and writhe,
    gurgling through the barbs in your throttle
Like a woolly caterpillar pinned on its back—man, that
    would be sweet.

     L. A. MACKAY

What makes you angry? Things you can do something about and things you can't. You get angry when you get a raw deal, when your best friend gets a raw deal, or when, because of war or pollution, the whole world gets a raw deal. Most of all, you get angry at people—at people you don't like and at people you do. You get angry at people you don't even know, like the girl who pushes you on a bus and the people who dump chemicals in the river where you swim.

In the first of the following two poems, the writer is angry at someone near at hand; in the second, the anger is directed against people unseen and unknown.

Black All Day

This morning, when he looked at me,
I saw how black I was
though there was nothing I could see
to give him any cause.

But I was black all day, and mean;
and leaving none to doubt,
I showed all day what I had seen
this morning stepping out.

He looked me into rage and shame;
no less, the day was grim.
Tomorrow, by another name,
I'll do as much for him.

RAYMOND R. PATTERSON

Above the Moving River

He saw the gas bubbles as
a boy, staring down
at the river from the city
bridge

and never guessed that
    as he grew into manhood
this river and city—
    this very country of
his birth, would fall
    into decline and ruin
and total destruction;
    that he would have to follow
these factory-spilled
    waters beyond the city
limits, and beyond this
    state, and then at last
beyond this country,
    if he was ever to keep
his boyhood and his
    manhood and his children
alive.

DAVID KHERDIAN

Loneliness is a quieter feeling than anger, and less sudden. It creeps in slowly like a silent mist, and it can pass by in a moment or linger for weeks. It appears when you are alone and abandoned or when you are in the middle of a noisy crowd. If you were to paint its picture, you would choose quiet, gentle colors—grays, maybe, or pale lavenders—and if you were to record its music, you would use quiet, reedy notes. Loneliness is a favorite subject of poets, maybe because writing poetry is a welcome pastime to the lonely. Some poets write of the loneliness they feel, and others of the loneliness they see. In the following poem the writer tells of the loneliness he feels:

Number 5—December

Nobody knows me
when I go round
late at night
scratching on windows
& whispering in hallways
looking for someone
who loves me in the daytime
to take me in
at night

DAVID HENDERSON

Another poet sees loneliness in a scene where he isn't present at all:

The Loon

A lonely lake, a lonely shore,
A lone pine leaning on the moon;
All night the water-beating wings
Of a solitary loon.

With mournful wail from dusk to dawn
He gibbered at the taunting stars—
A hermit-soul gone raving mad
And beating at his bars.

LEW SARETT

Try to remember a time when you were new in school or lost in a strange place. What did you do? What did you wish you could do? Sometimes it is easier to put your feelings into a picture, the way Lew Sarett did in his poem about the loon. Imagine a barren beach, an empty field, a bleak sky, a deserted street. Add a single detail that stands out against the bare background—a broken shell on the sand, a leafless tree in the meadow, a gull circling in the fog, a stray dog on the sidewalk. Set your poem in a lonely season at a lonely hour. You may, if you like, put yourself in the scene you create.

Fear can come on all at once, or it can come a little at a time. It can come in response to the real things and people of your everyday life or it can come from the world of make-believe. When it does come, it strikes at every part of your body—your heart, your teeth, your knees, your belly. It leaves you speechless or it makes you scream. It leaves you frozen or it makes you run.

For all that, people like to be frightened now and again, to shiver at the sight of a trembling curtain on the movie screen. People like, also, to frighten—to hide behind the curtain and make somebody else shiver. You don't need a movie camera to make a scary scene. A poem will do. A door can open as silently in a poem as on film, and insects can scuttle as swiftly across the floor. Shutters can bang and chimneys howl. More: the smell of cold ashes can hang in the air, icy cobwebs can break against the skin, the poisonous taste of a stale room can moisten the tongue.

William Shakespeare composed a "horror movie" long before the camera was invented:

> Now the hungry lion roars,
>   And the wolf behowls the moon;
> Whilst the heavy ploughman snores,
>   All with weary task fordone.

Now the wasted brands do glow,
　　Whilst the screech-owl, screeching loud,
Puts the wretch that lies in woe
　　In remembrance of a shroud.
Now it is the time of night,
　　That the graves, all gaping wide,
Every one lets forth his sprite,
　　In the church-way paths to glide. . . .

　　　WILLIAM SHAKESPEARE,
　　　A MIDSUMMER NIGHT'S DREAM, ACT V, SCENE I

If you were asked to draw up a list of all the things that made you mad and another of all the things that made you happy, you might find that the mad list was a good deal longer than the happy list. That's not because you're a grouch. Feelings of hate and anger have a way of announcing themselves more strongly than feelings of happiness, which are quieter and may pass by unnoticed. You don't often whisper to yourself "I'm happy" the way you tell yourself that you're scared or angry, and you may not realize how happy you really are until much later, when your memory tells you so.

Still, your life has its joyful moments, and they can be turned into joyful poetry. Getting a new bicycle can make you happy, and learning to ride it can make you even happier. Loving somebody—a boy or a girl, your mother or your father, or a movie star you've seen only on the screen and on magazine covers—can make you happy, and being loved back can make you happier still. You can be happy for no reason at all: you suddenly feel good and you tingle all over.

Many joyful poems are written about small moments of

happiness rather than about long periods of undefined good feeling. The first of the next two poems is about the beginning of spring, the next about a tumult of snow-flakes. Simple enough things, yet each poem describes an instant of joy and makes it, somehow, permanent.

Spring

I'm shouting
I'm singing
I'm swinging through trees
I'm winging sky-high
With the buzzing black bees.
I'm the sun
I'm the moon
I'm the dew on the rose.
I'm a rabbit
Whose habit
Is twitching his nose.
I'm lively
I'm lovely
I'm kicking my heels.
I'm crying "Come dance"
to the freshwater eels.
I'm racing through meadows
Without any coat
I'm a gamboling lamb
I'm a light leaping goat
I'm a bud
I'm a bloom
I'm a dove on the wing.
I'm running on rooftops
And welcoming spring!

KARLA KUSKIN

Winter Poem

once a snowflake fell
on my brow and i loved
it so much and i kissed
it and it was happy and called its cousins
and brothers and a web
of snow engulfed me then
i reached to love them all
and i squeezed them and they became
a spring rain and i stood perfectly
still and was a flower

NIKKI GIOVANNI

Maybe you spend more time wishing for happy moments than actually knowing them. Such wishes can be
turned into poems too. Suppose you could make the
whole world different for one day. Everybody would suddenly be nice to you. You could have all the bicycles and
pizzas you wanted. Everybody under the age of fifteen
would sprout wings. What would you wish? Here is what
one poet would do to make the world wonderful for one
day:

A Black Poetry Day

i am waiting for
a day when thousands
will gather before
shops and stores.

i am waiting for
a day when thousands
of BLACKS will listen
to the words of BLACK POETS.

i am waiting for
a BLACK POETRY DAY.

ALICIA LOY JOHNSON

Some of your feelings may stay with you a long time, seemingly forever, and others may come and go in a flash. They may get all mixed together; you may feel happy and lonely at the same time and you may hate someone even while you love him. But your feelings are yours alone. No one feels exactly the way you feel, and that is why no one else can write a poem exactly like yours.

15
Imagery

Reading a poem is often like viewing the sky on the Fourth of July. Sudden bursts of color explode upon the stillness, sometimes in rapid-fire succession, sometimes in single flashes, but always taking us by surprise and always making us gasp. We can be drowsing in the tranquillity of a stanza when suddenly something startling and wonderful illuminates its quiet. We will pause, and catch our breath, and send our eye back to the start of the line, so we can experience it all over again—which is one thing we can't do when we watch fireworks.

These sudden bursts of color often arise from passages where the poet presents us with something altogether familiar—a chimney, a bird, the moon, a potato—and with a sudden twist of words makes us see it as we have never seen it before.

In the following fragment from his poem "The Great Scarf of Birds," the American writer John Updike shows us some trees full of apples, and makes us stop dead in our tracks at the sight:

Ripe apples were caught like red fish in the nets
of their branches.

JOHN UPDIKE

The scattering of red apples against a tangle of
branches, an ordinary enough scene, takes on a new and
peculiar beauty when it is made to look like a group
of red fish in an open-weave net. Our minds, when we
read such a line, become like double-exposed film,
receiving impressions of apples and fish together,
where the web of the branches becomes the web of
the net and the red of the apples becomes the red of
the fish. Suddenly, the apple tree is touched by magic;
it takes on the characteristics of those trick pictures
on billboards or on trinkets in Cracker Jack boxes,
where with a sideways shift of the head we can see either
one scene or another, or, if we catch them just right,
both together: apples and red fish in one enchanted
display.

The art of describing something by showing how it
resembles something quite different is called *imagery*.
When a poet writes that apples in a tree look like fish in
a net, he is creating an *image*. For as long as poets have
been singing their songs and putting them in writing,
they have enriched their lines with the delights of imagery. William Shakespeare, writing four hundred years
ago, filled his plays and poems and songs with brilliant,
haunting, and unforgettable comparisons and like-
nesses. Here are two:

Night's candles are burnt out, and jocund day
Stands tiptoe on the misty mountain tops.

WILLIAM SHAKESPEARE,
ROMEO AND JULIET, ACT III, SCENE 5

. . . Kate like the hazel-twig
Is straight and slender, and as brown in hue
As hazel-nuts and sweeter than the kernels.

WILLIAM SHAKESPEARE,
TAMING OF THE SHREW, ACT II, SCENE I

Fifteen hundred years ago a Chinese poet embellished
his poem with this image:

from *Ruined City*

A solitary reed shakes and twists,
And grains of sand, like startled birds,
     are looking for a safe place to settle.

PAO CHAO
(TRANSLATED BY JEROME CH'ÊN
AND MICHAEL BULLOCK)

Three thousand years ago, the Greek poet Homer, in
his epic poems *The Iliad* and *The Odyssey*, used frequent
images to describe the sea and the sky and the lovely
golden sandals that bore the messenger Hermes over sea
and land, "swift as the breath of wind."

Imagery is not the language of the poet alone. We use
it all the time in our everyday speech. When we say that
Jim eats like a horse or is as sly as a fox or that the rabbit's

fur is as soft as silk, we may not realize it but we are speaking with images. Sometimes it is impossible not to. How can anyone describe the cry of a cat, for instance, or the blue of a feather, without putting it side by side with something else and saying, "This is like that"?

Yet some imagery is poetry and some is not. The image "Jim eats like a horse" is so much a part of our daily speech that when we hear it, we barely respond to it at all. We know at once that Jim has a pretty big appetite, but we don't have to think much about the horse to understand that. Something special, however, happens when we read the following image by the twentieth-century English poet Humbert Wolfe: "Like a small grey coffee-pot sits the squirrel." Now, instead of one picture, we see two—one of a squirrel and one of a coffeepot—and each magically changes the other. The squirrel, an ordinary creature just a moment before, is transformed before our eyes into something we never dreamed it could be: a small gray coffeepot. And at the same time, the coffeepot comes to life and settles itself in the branches of a tree. That is the magic of imagery.

To perform magic like this, writers go through a very personal experience. They begin with a single subject—a squirrel, say, or apples in a tree. Then they reach back into their private store of remembered things and choose from it a matching picture—a coffeepot for a squirrel or red fish for apples. It is a picture that is theirs alone. Sometimes it comes up in a flash, sometimes writers must search for it at length. Always, though, they look for their pictures within themselves. That is what Shakespeare did. It's what Pao Chao did, and it's what Homer did. You can do it, too.

Go out of doors and wander around a bit. Look along the sidewalk, or in a doorway, or on a lawn, for something you can pick up. It doesn't have to be a squirrel; a withered leaf, all green and yellow, will do just as well. Bring it inside and set it down in front of you. Look at it as though you had never seen a withered green-and-yellow leaf before in your whole life. What does it make you think of? Start with its colors. Green and yellow. Reach back into *your* private store of remembered things for pictures that match the yellow and green on the leaf. You've seen lots of yellow things, and lots of green things, and lots of yellow-and-green things. Get your notebook and write down every single one you can think of: yellow butter and yellow butterflies and yellow mittens and yellow beads and yellow fish and yellow lemon drops and yellow paper towels and a yellow sun. Green soda bottles and green frogs and green seesaws and green cat eyes and green giants. Green-and-yellow tie-dyed shirts and green-and-yellow pinwheels and green-and-yellow turtle bellies and green-and-yellow snakes and green and yellow Play-Doh that got mixed together by mistake.

Don't worry if your images aren't beautiful or "poetic." If a yellow leaf makes you think of a butterfly wing or the sun, that's quite lovely, but if it reminds you of something in your sock drawer, that can be quite lovely, too. Lovelier, really, because chances are no one else would have thought that up, and when a thought is special to you, it becomes special to your readers as well.

Now put your list aside for a while and go back to your leaf. This time examine its shape or its design. If it's old and dry, it might be curled up like a cup. Or a shell. Or a rowboat. Or a baby's hand or a soup bowl or a potato chip. Return to your notebook and write down whatever comes into your head. "The leaf is curled up like a _____." Or "flat as a _____" (not pancake—somebody's already thought that one up). "It's jagged as a _____."

What else? Run your thumb along its surface, scratch it with your fingernail, smooth it against your cheek. What are all the things you have ever felt that are brittle and rough like your withered leaf? Something you ate for breakfast? Some old leather thing you once wore? Somebody's face? Write them down: "a leaf as dry as a corn-flake," "a leaf as brittle as an old leather glove," "a leaf as wrinkled as my great-grandpa's face." Some leaves become smooth and shiny as they dry out, like patent-leather pocketbooks or sneaker soles. If that's what your leaf is like, try to think of all the things you have ever known that are smooth and shiny. Write them down in your notebook.

Now, place the leaf on the floor and give it a good enough puff of wind to set it skimming across the room. What else moves like that? Ballerinas and wind-up toys and frightened birds? Stand on a chair with your leaf and be a tree for a moment. With a twist of your fingers, release the last of your autumn foliage, letting it slowly float to the ground. What are some other things that float like that? Things with wings do, and things on strings, and things with sails. Write down whatever comes into your head.

And now for the end of your leaf. Take it in your hand and crumble it hard. Listen! What did that sound like? What crunchy things have you bitten into, what crackly things have you crushed, what crispy things have you stepped on that sound like the leaf breaking against your hand?

Look over your lists now and pick out those images that you like best. Your favorites will probably be those that no one but you could have thought up. Arrange some of them on a new page in your notebook and read them aloud. You might find, to your surprise, that you have already written a poem. Some poetry is just that: a whole string of images called up by the color or shape or feel or sound of one special thing. A ten-year-old boy wrote such a poem about a razor clam shell:

Razor Clam Shell

It feels like old concrete beginning to chip.
It is a tremendous finger.
It is covered with the scribbling of chalk
Or the splatters of paint.
Its curved claw looks like
Half a rowboat
In the splashing water.

BRETT YOCHES

And Hilda Conkling, a poet whose first collection of poems was published in 1920 when she was ten, made up a whole group of images about a rooster:

Red Rooster

Red rooster in your gray coop,
O stately creature with tail-feathers red and blue,
Yellow and black,
You have a comb gay as a parade
On your head:
You have pearl trinkets
On your feet:
The short feathers smooth along your back
Are the dark color of wet rocks,
Or the rippled green of ships
When I look at their sides through water.
I don't know how you happened to be made
So proud, so foolish
Wearing your coat of many colors,
Shouting all day long your crooked words,
Loud . . . sharp . . . not beautiful!

HILDA CONKLING

Images come in many forms. The easiest to compose, because it is closest to the way we talk, is the simple comparison that you have just been reading and making up yourself. The apples are like fish, the squirrel is like a coffeepot, the razor-clam shell is like half a rowboat. Such an image, where one object is said to be "like" another, is called a *simile*, and it is the most common form of imagery.

Sometimes, though, all those "likes" become monotonous and clumsy after a while, and writers look for other kinds of word arrangements to express their imagery. Instead of saying that the leaf is *like* a butterfly, for example, they might simply say that the leaf *is* a butterfly. "The leaf is a golden butterfly," maybe, "quivering at the end of a branch." An image that, instead of comparing two things, makes one thing another is called a *metaphor*. The apples *are* fish, the squirrel *is* a coffeepot, the razor-clam shell *is* half a rowboat. In the following metaphor, a toaster is a dragon:

from *The Toaster*

A silver-scaled Dragon with jaws flaming red
Sits at my elbow and toasts my bread.

WILLIAM JAY SMITH

An entire poem can be one metaphor:

The Garden Hose

In the gray evening
I see a long green serpent
With its tail in the dahlias.

It lies in loops across the grass
And drinks softly at the faucet.

I can hear it swallow.

BEATRICE JANOSCO

Or a poem can be a whole group of separate metaphors:

Ballet School

Fawns in the winter wood
Who feel their horns, and leap,
Swans whom the bleakening mood
Of evening stirs from sleep,
Tall flowers that unfurl
As a moth, driven, flies,
Flowers with the breast of a girl
And sea-cold eyes.
The bare bright mirrors glow
For their enchanted shapes.
Each is a flame, and so,
Like flame, escapes.

BABETTE DEUTSCH

In the preceding poem, the author transformed a
group of people into animals and birds and flowers.
Very often a poet will do just the opposite and transform animals and birds and flowers—or anything else
nonhuman—into people. Things that have no faces
will smile, and things that have no legs will skip.
Things that have no wardrobes will put on their
gowns, and things that have no voices will sing. The
wind will whimper, the sun will paint the evening sky,
the trees will don their scarlet shawls, the angry sea
will shout. Imagery in which objects are given human
characteristics is called *personification*, and it is still an-

other means of heightening a description by creating a double picture.

Here is a poem where all the images are personifications—fences have hats, bushes have knees, and trees wear dance clothes:

Snow

The fenceposts wear marshmallow hats
On a snowy day;
Bushes in their night gowns
Are kneeling down to pray—
And all the trees have silver skirts
And want to dance away.

DOROTHY ALDIS

Some images are found in single words. An adjective, a noun, or a verb can create an image all by itself. Like "the baby's *pumpkin* cheeks," for example, or "a *whisker* of a moon," or "the squirrel *feather-dusted* the branch." Try to find the images almost hidden among the words in the following verses:

from Kangaroo

So she wistfully, sensitively sniffs the air,
        and then turns, goes off in slow sad leaps

On the long flat skis of her legs,
Steered and propelled by that steel-strong snake of a tail.

D. H. LAWRENCE

from *Dolphin Seen Alone*

One dolphin.
                Strongly curved, watertight
and snug, zippered in
to suit of dark green skin
he sprouts and plunges. Bulk and blunt snout bite
gunmetal gray water, and no land's in sight.

RICHMOND LATTIMORE

Now, let's get back to your poem. Look over your list
of remembered things once more and turn them into
new kinds of images. Some can remain similes, of course,
but others can become metaphors, and still others can be
made into personifications, with feet or fingers or a voice
or a suit of clothes. Catch your reader unawares and hide
an image in an adjective or a noun. Instead of "The leaf
crackles like a gum wrapper," try something like "The
leaf with its gum-wrapper crackle. . . ." Whatever its
form—simile, metaphor, personification—your image, if
it is a good one, will have the effect upon your readers
of forming in their minds a double picture of things that
are altogether different and yet oddly the same.

It won't always be necessary to pick something up and
carry it indoors in order to create images about it. Nor
will it always be possible; you can't conveniently set a sea
gull on the kitchen table. In time, though, you will find
that images come to mind as things strike your eye. A
row of birds on a telephone wire or the midnight cry of
a cat will bring up sudden pictures from your memory
that can become instant poems. For that matter, you

don't have to see or hear an object at all. Close your eyes
and *imagine* one. It doesn't have to belong to the world
of flowers, and leaves, and sunsets, either; footballs and
trash cans make good images too.

The important thing is that your images have to be
special to *you*. They must come from *your* store of remembered things. The pictures that are filed away in
your head are as real as those of any poet's. But to collect
all those pictures in the first place, you must take time to
watch things, to listen to them and feel them and smell
them and roll them about on your tongue. Whatever you
pick up and hold in your hand today is a remembered
thing for tomorrow, and there you have a poem—a poem
that is all yours, forever.

16

Who Am I?
Riddle Poems

An image tells us, "This thing is like that thing." Sometimes, though, a poet will use an image to play a guessing game and ask *"What* thing is like that thing?" telling his reader all along what his subject is like, but never what it is. Instead of offering a complete image, he asks a riddle, sometimes to add mystery to his poem, but just as often to tease—for riddles are, more than anything else, fun. Asking one is like hiding something behind your back and saying, "Guess what I have! I'll give you three hints. . . ." Riddles are fun whether you are on the teasing end or the guessing end, whether you solve them or are stumped by them, and poets enjoy them as much as anybody else.

The riddle of poetry is not the "trick riddle" or When-is-a-door-not-a-door? variety, which depend on word-plays and surprise jokes. Rather, it is what is known as a "true riddle," one that offers a series of clues, often in rhyme, and then asks the unspoken question "Who am I?" True riddles have been around, in one form or another, for hundreds of years. You may remember this one from Mother Goose:

Thirty white horses upon a red hill.
Now they tramp, now they champ, now they stand still.*

MOTHER GOOSE

The next, also from Mother Goose, is trickier. Each line contains a mystery all its own, and only when you have solved the whole riddle do the separate metaphors make sense.

In marble halls as white as milk,
Lined with skin as soft as silk,
Within a fountain crystal clear,
A golden apple doth appear.
No doors there are to this stronghold,
Yet thieves break in and steal the gold.†

MOTHER GOOSE

Riddle poems such as these are meant to be recited just as a game. They are more riddle than poem. But others, by poets who are concerned with language and imagery as well as with keeping a secret, are as much poem as riddle. They offer a double pleasure—the beauty of poetry and the joy of discovery. The following poem would be a fine one even if its author had not hidden its subject from her readers. Its riddle, though, is a good one, and difficult; although many so-

---

*Teeth.
†An egg.

lutions seem to apply, there's only one that fits all the clues.

> I like to see it lap the miles,
> And lick the valleys up,
> And stop to feed itself at tanks;
> And then, prodigious, step
>
> Around a pile of mountains,
> And, supercilious, peer
> In shanties by the sides of roads;
> And then a quarry pare
>
> To fit its sides, and crawl between,
> Complaining all the while
> In horrid, hooting stanza;
> Then chase itself down hill
>
> And neigh like Boanerges;
> Then, punctual as a star,
> Stop—docile and omnipotent—
> At its own stable door.‡

EMILY DICKINSON

Writing a riddle poem of your own is no harder than writing an image. In fact, they are the same thing. Begin by contemplating an object—its color, its action, its shape, its sound, its smell, its taste—and match it with something that is quite the same and yet totally different. A tree in autumn, for instance, might remind you of a molting bird—a bird shedding its feathers. If you were

---

‡A train. ("Boanerges" means a noisy preacher.)

to put such an image into conventional poetry, it might come out like this:

> The autumn tree
> is a molting bird,
> dropping its orange feathers
> to the ground.

To convert this image into a riddle poem, keep the tree a secret. Tell only what it is like, not what it is:

> I am a molting bird;
> my feathers, orange and red,
> drop gently to the ground.

Usually, one clue is not enough to solve a riddle. A really good riddle can have only one answer, so you must provide enough clues to eliminate all other possibilities. In the riddle poem above, further clues, suggesting the branches waving like wings, perhaps, would have to be offered. In the following poem the first two lines alone might apply to several insects, but the third line narrows it down to only one:

One Guess

> He has dust in his eyes and a fan for a wing,
> A leg akimbo with which he can sing,
> And a mouthful of dye stuff instead of a sting.*

ROBERT FROST

---

*A grasshopper.

The best riddle subjects are those with special characteristics that set them apart from all other things. Choose one that is likely to be familiar to most readers and that can be turned into a good metaphor. A firefly, with its signaling flashlight, might be good. So would an oyster, which may hide a jewel within its jaws; a snail, which travels about in its own camper truck; and a snake, which removes its overcoat and drops it on the ground.

Objects that undergo transformations make good riddle subjects too, because a clue can be provided for each change. The moon, for example, which one night is a silver eyebrow and another a brass dish, is a good subject for a riddle, and so are a caterpillar, which becomes a ballerina, and a snowman, which is a jolly fellow one day and a sorry puddle the next.

If your subject has many characteristics, you may want to write a separate metaphor for each. If you choose a rattlesnake, for instance, think up one metaphor for its darting tongue, another for the rattles on its tail, and still another for the poison in its bite. Here is an example of a riddle poem with many images:

Living Tenderly

My body a rounded stone
with a pattern of smooth seams.
My head a short snake,
retractive, projective.
My legs come out of their sleeves
or shrink within,
and so does my chin.
My eyelids are quick clamps.

My back is my roof.
I am always at home.
I travel where my house walks.
It is a smooth stone.
It floats within the lake,
or rests in the dust.
My flesh lives tenderly
inside its bone.†

MAY SWENSON

   Or you may stick to one giant metaphor made up of
many smaller parts. Maybe autumn reminds you of a
tremendous Halloween party: the trees are children in
gypsy clothes, the sun is a fat jack-o'-lantern burning in
the sky, the fallen leaves are cast-off candy wrappers.
Your poem would tell only of the party, the costumes,
the jack-o'-lantern, and the candy wrappers, leaving your
reader to puzzle out each detail.

   Your riddle poem can ask "Who am I?" or it can ask
"Who is he?" It can be tricky or it can be easy. It can have
many metaphors or it can have only one. Keep in mind,
though, that a riddle poem is exactly that—a poem that
is a riddle. Write it like a poem. Use the language of
poetry. Develop your metaphor carefully and then, once
it is perfect, keep half of it a secret, for that is what a true
riddle is: a metaphor with one half held behind your
back.

---

†A turtle.

17

Haiku

People everywhere dream up poems. On every continent and in every century, someone suddenly has something wonderful to say and says it in words that are chosen as though they were flowers for a bouquet—with care.

Very often poets thousands of miles apart will tell of the same wonderful thing. But the poems themselves—their style, their shape, whatever it is that tells the listener "This is a poem"—vary widely from culture to culture, just as styles in shoes and hairdos do. The poem of India is altogether unlike the poem of Africa, although both may serenade the same man in the same moon, and the poem of America is unlike the poem of Japan.

Here are two poems, one a Mother Goose rhyme that you will remember, the other a less familiar poem from Japan. They tell the same story: someone is being paid a visit by a bug. But notice in what different ways they tell it. First the Mother Goose:

Little Miss Muffet
Sat on a tuffet
Eating her curds and whey;
Along came a spider,
Who sat down beside her,
And frightened Miss Muffet away.

MOTHER GOOSE

Now the Japanese:

Red dragonfly on
my shoulder calls me his friend.
Autumn has arrived.

SOSEKI
(TRANSLATED BY SYLVIA CASSEDY
AND KUNIHIRO SUETAKE)

We easily recognize the nursery rhyme as a poem because it contains what we are used to hearing in poetry—a set of agreeable rhymes and a rhythm that we can clap out. But the Japanese verse doesn't seem to be a poem at all. It looks incomplete, and it is over the moment it is begun. Yet it has a pattern of its own, and a Japanese would know at once that it was a poem.

The Japanese verse belongs to a class of poetry known as *haiku* (pronounced "HIGH-koo"), an ancient form dating back to the thirteenth century and still flourishing in Japan today. Although haiku poetry is short and seems easy to read, it is filled with hidden, and often difficult, meaning, and it is actually studied in Japan more by adults than by children.

Its form, too, is difficult. It is based not on rhyming words or steady rhythms, but on the number of syllables in each line. Counting on your fingers now, read the haiku about the dragonfly again and tick off the number of syllables in each line. You will find that the first line contains five syllables, the next seven, and the third five again. Five-seven-five: that is the form that identifies such poetry as haiku.

Why syllables? We don't pay much attention to English syllables, because it is difficult to separate them from the words they form. In Japanese, however, the syllable is a distinct unit, with only one consonant sound to each vowel. It often has a meaning all its own. The word *hotaru*, for instance, which means "firefly," is easily divided into three separate sounds: ho-ta-ru. The syllables of *firefly*, on the other hand, are not so well defined; it is hard to tell where one ends and the next begins.

What's more, it is easier to fit a thought into a handful of syllables in Japanese than it is in English, because our language uses a great many words that Japanese does without. Our sentences need such words as "the," "a," "that," "which," "he," and "she" in order to make sense. In Japanese these words are usually unnecessary.

Then why try to write haiku in English at all? Because composing a haiku is more than an exercise in arranging words into groups of syllables. The following set of words is organized into three lines with a total of seventeen syllables, but it isn't a haiku:

>The plane from New York
>will touch down at Chicago
>at five forty-five.

Haiku is an experience of the eye and of the heart, and cumbersome as the English language may sometimes seem to be, there are words within it that can capture this experience for us as brilliantly as the syllables of Japanese can for the poet of Japan.

A haiku is a tiny picture in words. Each syllable is like the sweep of a brush in a Japanese ink sketch. And, like the sketch, with its few, quick strokes and bare background, a haiku suggests things rather than describes them. There are few details. A haiku poet will pick from the landscape only one or two fragments—a grasshopper on a leaf, maybe, or a frog on a stone—and leave all the rest unspoken.

Imagine, as an example, a summer night filled with the silent flashes of a thousand fireflies. An American poet of this century and a poet writing over two hundred years ago in Japan each composed a poem in response to just such a night. This is the American poem:

from *Fireflies*

>Oh, who is lost tonight?
>The field and garden are alight
>With tiny lanterns, bobbing, winking,
>High in the soundless boughs or sinking,
>A-flicker in the forests of the grass.

All through the night they pass,
Silently peering with their cheerful torches
In snails' round doors, and spiders' ruined porches,
Blowing a patient spark
In every corner of the dark.

WINIFRED WELLES

And this is the poem from Japan:

As I pick it up
to cage it . . . the firefly
lights my fingertips.

TAIGI
(EDITED BY SYLVIA CASSEDY)

The American poem, with its multitude of details, resembles a still-life painting by a Dutch master, where the canvas is crowded with flowers, fruit, jewels, and insects, all painted in perfect imitation of the real bouquet that must have stood on the real table before the artist's easel. The artist, like the American poet, offered his audience everything he saw.

The haiku, on the other hand, contains only two details—one firefly and a pair of fingertips—chosen from a vast and busy night. It is the reader who must supply the background and fill in the outlines, reaching into his own memories of firefly-filled nights to supply the full moon, the row of shadowy pine trees on the horizon, or the faint smell of bug repellent on the air. Such a poem is like a Japanese watercolor, where only a bamboo stalk and its scattering of down-turned leaves decorate the paper. The sky, the ground, the distant hills that may

have appeared before the artist's eye remain unde-
scribed. Yet someone familiar with Japanese painting
will know immediately that the drooping leaves suggest
rain, although not a drop of rain appears, and will supply
from his imagination the puddles and umbrellas the artist left out.

The next three haiku are like the bamboo watercolor.
There is more meaning in what is left untold than in what
declares itself to the eye. Read each poem a few times.
After each reading, close your eyes and add details to the
scene as though you were finishing a picture in a coloring
book where only the outline of a housetop is provided,
or the back of a cat.

> Good morning, sparrow,
> writing on my clean veranda
> with your dewy feet.
>
> SHIKI

> The floating heron
> pecks at it till it shatters . . .
> full-moon-on-water.
>
> ZUIRYU

> The night is hot . . .
> Stripped to the waist, the snail
> enjoys the moonlight.
>
> ISSA
> (EDITED BY SYLVIA CASSEDY)

A haiku poet who singles out one firefly from the swarm or one sparrow from the flock is expressing an ancient Japanese idea: every object, however small, is important both to its neighbor and to itself. A Japanese flower arrangement may contain only three elements—a chrysanthemum, a pine branch, and a spray of oak leaves. Each element is valued for its beauty and for the effect it has on the whole design. If you took away one element, the arrangement would be ruined. In our culture, we are more accustomed to larger groupings of flowers, where the removal of one blossom would go unnoticed, and of course such groupings are beautiful too, but they do not express the Japanese idea of beauty.

So far in these haiku we have met a firefly, a sparrow, a snail, a heron, a dragonfly, and the moon. That is the world of haiku. A haiku is a nature poem. It is a poem of the seasons, of things that sleep under the summer sun or quiver against the autumn sky, of things that stir in the springtime earth or shiver in the winter wind.

The haiku poet chooses a single firefly from the swarm—and then chooses a single moment out of the firefly's life to capture in poetry. One single moment. And not just any moment; it must be a special one, when the firefly is doing something more exciting than what it was doing a moment before or than what it will be doing a moment from now. The poet calls this the "high moment," and no well-written haiku is without it. It is like the moment you wait for when you are wandering about with your camera. For a long time, nothing happens. Then suddenly two swans on a lake form a perfect heart with their necks, you raise your camera to your eye, and you snap the shutter. That is a high moment. It is the moment when the *poet* snaps the shutter, capturing in words what you have caught on film:

> Face to face,
> two swans swim together,
> like a valentine.

> LAURA SHTRICK (AGE NINE)

Sometimes a high moment is achieved when two opposites appear against one another—something black on something white, something bumpy on something smooth, something soft on something hard. Here are some haiku whose beauty lies in just such contrasts:

> Bird droppings pattern
> the purples and yellows of
> my iris petals.

> BUSON

> The heavy wagon
> shakes all the roadside, waking
> a single butterfly.

> SHOHA

> Against the broad sky,
> stretching and leaning,
> winter trees.

> KYOSHI
> (TRANSLATED BY GEOFFREY BOWNAS
> AND ANTHONY THWAITE)

Creating a picture of contrasts might be a good way to begin your own haiku. Imagine a background—any good, clear expanse will do: a bare sky, a field of snow, a stretch of sand, or a stone wall. Now, place upon it a single object—a wheeling bird, a grasshopper, a twirling maple seed—that will both stand out against the background and allow the background to stand out against *it.* This is a little like choosing the right beads to wear on a sweater. Remember to select your subjects from the world of nature; birds and frogs make better material for haiku than skateboards.

Or you might want to start the other way around. Choose a living creature—a ladybug, say—and try her out on different surfaces until you have found one that just suits her polished shell. A sunflower petal, maybe, or the trunk of a birch. That alone—a bug on a petal or a tree—is quite enough material to work with, but you may want to choose one high moment out of her life to write about. A gust of wind might shake the flower stalk, taking her for an unexpected ride, or she might set out by herself on a brief journey across the white bark of the birch.

Now start putting your ideas on paper. Don't worry about syllables at this point, or even about sentences. Just set down some words and phrases. You won't use them all in your poem, but it's good to have many to choose from. Remember that you want your readers to *see* your picture. If your ladybug has rusty spots on her back, use a phrase like "red-spotted," "rust-spotted shell," or "rusted back." Avoid saying she's "pretty" or "nice." And if she's creeping from petal to petal, say that. Don't just say she's moving around.

Don't worry too much about the number of syllables. Although a haiku is defined as having a five-seven-five syllable pattern, not all haiku, even in Japanese, follow the rule strictly, so don't alter the meaning of your poem just to make the syllables fit. Try to keep *close* to five-seven-five, though. A first or third line of fewer than three syllables would be too short, and a middle line of nine or ten syllables would be too long. Keep a nice balance. If your first line has three syllables, your middle line would seem too long if it had as many as eight. If you are having trouble with the wording, try rearranging the order of ideas. Put the last line first, maybe, or the middle line last.

Many haiku are in the form of metaphors, and you might want to convert some of the images you thought up earlier into haiku. Here are some examples:

> Morning-misted street—
> with white ink an artist brushes
> a dream of people.
>
> BUSON

> Up the barley rows,
> stitching, stitching them together,
> a butterfly goes.
>
> SORA
> (TRANSLATED BY HAROLD G. HENDERSON)

Cardinal on the snow—
a berry on a white sheet
in the winter cold.

ADAM CARLSON (AGE EIGHT)

Not all haiku are solemn. Some are silly:

A discovery!
On my frog's smooth, green belly
there sits no button.

YAYU
(TRANSLATED BY SYLVIA CASSEDY
AND KUNIHIRO SUETAKE)

Whatever your subject, there are a few rules to keep in mind when you write haiku.

First, limit your poem to one or two subjects. A sea gull on a rock should be all you need for a beach scene.

Second, keep yourself out of the picture. Very few Japanese haiku contain the pronoun "I." Think of yourself once again as a photographer, recording only what you see. Or hear, for that matter; a haiku can be about the belch of a frog or the scratch of a claw.

Next, make your poem happen right at this moment— now. The squirrel *rubs* its nose; not *rubbed*. Make it happen all at once. The squirrel rubs its nose as the raindrops fall, not the raindrops fall and then, after a while, the squirrel rubs its nose.

In time, you may decide that what is important about a haiku is its feeling and not its rules about lines and syllables. Many recent poets have imitated the haiku style, but have chosen to ignore its form. Ezra Pound, the twentieth-century American poet, was one. He saved an important moment out of his life by reducing it to what he called "a haikulike sentence." He had just stepped off a train in the Paris subway—or Métro, as it is called there—when there appeared before him a succession of beautiful faces, one after another. A beautiful woman's face here, a beautiful child's face there, one by one they flashed before his eyes, and he was so struck by the sight that he wanted to preserve its memory forever. He did so in two lines and fourteen words:

In a Station of the Métro

The apparition of these faces in the crowd;
Petals on a wet, black bough.

EZRA POUND

Such a poem has all the elements of a haiku except for the arrangement of lines and syllables. Raymond R. Patterson also composed a poem that is haikulike in feeling but not quite in form:

Glory, Glory . . .

Across Grandmother's knees
A kindly sun
Laid a yellow quilt.

RAYMOND R. PATTERSON

The following two American poems, with their single strokes of color, contain the precise feeling of Japanese picture poems, even though they don't resemble haiku in form. In "The Red Wheelbarrow," when the poet suggests that without the red of the wet wheelbarrow the white chickens would be lost in the landscape, he is stating the same idea expressed in the Japanese flower arrangement, where the chrysanthemum is essential to the evergreen branch against which it is placed.

The Red Wheelbarrow

so much depends
upon

a red wheel
barrow

glazed with rain
water

beside the white
chickens

WILLIAM CARLOS WILLIAMS

And in "Snow Country," the vast, white Wyoming landscape takes on new importance when it is splotched with the sudden yellow of a school bus.

Snow Country

only
a little
yellow

school bus
creeping along
a thin

ribbon
of snow road
splashed color

on the white
winter canvas
that was

Wyoming
from the train
yesterday

DAVE ETTER

Now read the following Japanese haiku, written more than half a century earlier. In it, a scattering of red berries has the same effect on its background as the wheelbarrow in the chicken yard and the school bus in the snow:

See the red berries
fallen like little footprints
on the garden snow.

SHIKI

The twentieth-century poet Richard Aldridge, like all the haiku poets of Japan, created a grand event out of a single fragment plucked from the landscape:

The Pine Bough

I saw a thing, and stopped to wonder—
For who had set the moment when
The pine bough should dip out from under
The white oppressor's arm of snow,
And upward fling itself, as though
Attracted to a blue May heaven?

RICHARD ALDRIDGE

"Seeing a thing and stopping to wonder" is what haiku is all about. If you can preserve that thing in three lines and seventeen syllables, that is wonderful. If you can preserve it in several stanzas of rhymed verse or in a twenty-five-word sentence, that is wonderful too.

18

Words That Whisper, Words That Sing

Words are magic—the instant you hear one, a picture enters your head. Hear the word *spinach*—there in your head is a bowl of spinach, green juice and all. Words are like buttons on a superspecial picture-making machine. Push one down, up pops a picture. Any word that you hear or see stirs something in your mind. That is what communication is all about.

But some words are even more magic than that. They can put pictures in your mind without your even knowing what they mean, not by what they say, but by how they sound. Some words sound like thunder, some words sound like pillows, and some words sound like putting your hands in mashed potatoes. Try it. Here are some nonsense words; they have no meaning in English, and yet, when spoken aloud, some sound like soft, whispery things and others sound like noisy, rough things. Which ones put quiet pictures in your head? which noisy? *Ploor. Lollow. Jankle. Chizzick. Shrull. Groggix.*

There are *real* words, too, that have soft sounds and loud sounds, regardless of their meanings. A foreigner hearing the word *thistle* for the first time might think it meant something soft and rustly, because it has a soft and rustly sound—*thistle*—even though it has a rough and prickly meaning. *Willow* has a quiet sound too. So do *shallow, slush, push, shawl,* and *plow.* Say them aloud and listen. *Crackers* has a loud sound, even when you whisper it. *Junk* sounds noisy too, and so do *grouch, clutch,* and *choke.*

Best of all are those words whose sound and meaning seem to go together: quiet words that have quiet meanings, noisy words that have noisy meanings. *Whisper, swish,* and *hush* all sound as quiet as a breath of wind. *Lullaby* and *plush* have sounds that are just right for their meanings. There are noisy words with noisy meanings: *break, jangle, strike, gargle.*

You have probably noticed that the soft-sounding words have letters or letter combinations like *sh, l, w, p, s, h, wh, th*; and loud-sounding words have such consonants as *k, sk, nk, ch, ng, j, g, x,* and *v.* Murmuring words have lots of *m*'s and *n*'s, and buzzing words have lots of *z*'s. (The words *murmur* and *buzz* belong to a special category. When you speak them aloud they make the very sound they mean. Naming a thing by the sound it makes is called *onomatopoeia* [pronounced "on-a-maht-a-PEA-a"]. *Hiss, crackle, rustle, jingle,* and *clink* are all examples of onomatopoeia.)

Now make up some nonsense words of your own. Change the underlined words in the following sentence into a new language whose words sound just like their meaning: "The *soft rain hit* the *beehive* in the *murmuring pines.*" Choose a quiet sound for *soft* and a plinking sound for *rain*, a banging sound for *hit*, a buzzy sound for *beehive*, a hummy sound for *murmur*, and a prickly sound for *pines.*

A poet describing a quiet, gentle scene will often select quiet, gentle words, just as a composer will choose quiet instruments playing quiet notes for a passage suggesting a quiet mood. And a poet describing a raucous scramble will use clamorous, jangling words that rattle in the ear.

Recite the next two poems aloud and listen as the words whisper like falling snow and twitter and croak like birds, bats, and frogs:

from *Velvet Shoes*

Let us walk in the white snow
In a soundless space;
With footsteps quiet and slow,
At a tranquil pace,
Under veils of white lace.

I shall go shod in silk,
And you in wool,
White as a white cow's milk,
More beautiful
Than the breast of a gull.

ELINOR WYLIE

from *The Sound of Night*

And now the dark comes on,
all full of chitter noise.
Birds huggermugger crowd the trees,
the air thick with their vesper cries,

and bats, snub seven-pointed kites,
skitter across the lake, swing out,
squeak, chirp, dip, and skim on skates
of air, and the fat frogs wake and prink
wide-lipped, noisy as ducks, drunk
on the boozy black, gloating chink-chunk.

MAXINE KUMIN

Imagine now a silent scene thick with fog. Everything looks as though it's been drawn in gray chalk. The houses have fuzzy outlines, trees look like X-ray pictures, telephone wires glisten with silver drops, and the air is heavy and still. Describe such a scene in a poem or, if you wish, a few sentences. Use words that are as still and silent and thick with fog as the picture you are describing. Or, instead, choose a garden full of bees, a thunderstorm in the woods, rain rushing in torrents down the street, an airport, or a football game. Let your words swish along with the rain or roar along with the crowd.

Words not only whisper and shout; they also leap and creep. Some words, especially those with short vowels and hard consonants, are quick and snappy; others, those with long vowels and soft consonants, are slow and lazy. The word *sprawl* takes longer to say than the word *tick*, even though each is one syllable long. Say the next group of words aloud. Each pair has an equal number of syllables, but one word in each is slow and the other fast. Which is which?

> *sip——croon*
> *moonglow——pickle*
> *bigwig——phone booth*
> *hula hoop——jitterbug*

Just as poets choose quiet sounds for quiet poems and noisy sounds for noisy poems, they will choose slow sounds for slow poems and quick sounds for quick poems. To describe the lightness of a rabbit's movements a poet will choose words like *hop, skip, skitter,* and *scud,* rather than slow-moving words like *vault* and *bound* and *lope.* An elephant out for a stroll would more likely *lumber* than *step*; if it lost its footing it would *sprawl* rather than *trip*; and if it decided not to get up for a while, it would *slumber* rather than *nap.* A lumbering, slumbering, sprawling elephant *sounds* bigger, heavier, and more elephantlike than a stepping, tripping, napping one.

Here is a poem about the ocean—vast, ponderous, slow. The words reflect the size and tempo of the sea, and it is almost impossible not to read them slowly:

Winter Ocean

Many-maned scud-thumper, tub
of male whales, maker of worn wood, shrub-
ruster, sky-mocker, rave!
portly pusher of waves, wind-slave.

JOHN UPDIKE

The next poem has all the scampering words of the cat that is its subject:

Cat!

Cat!
Scat!
After her, after her,
Sleeky flatterer,
Spitfire chatterer,
Scatter her, scatter her
   Off her mat!
   Wuff!
   Wuff!
   Treat her rough!
Git her, git her,
Whiskery spitter!
Catch her, catch her,
Green-eyed scratcher!
   Slathery
   Slithery
   Hisser,
   Don't miss her!
Run till you're dithery,
   Hithery
   Thithery
   Pftts! pftts!
   How she spits!
   Spitch! Spatch!
   Can't she scratch!
Scritching the bark
Of the sycamore-tree,
She's reached her ark
And's hissing at me
   Pftts! pftts!
   Wuff! wuff!

Scat,
Cat!
That's
That!

ELEANOR FARJEON

Think of a whale for a moment, big and lumpish in the water. Try to find ten slow, heavy, drawling words that sound the way it moves. Put some of them—or all of them, if you can—into a poem. Now try the same thing with a grasshopper.

Words whisper, words shout. Words leap, words creep. Words also sing. Repeat the following groups of words one after another, and listen to the music they make:

mumble tremble rumble scramble
thimble nimble jumble gamble
bramble humble tumble cymbal

Poets often use words that, when put together, sound like something that might come out of a musical instrument. The following poem sounds like the warbling of a flute:

Counting-Out Rhyme

Silver bark of beech, and sallow
Bark of yellow birch and yellow
   Twig of willow.

Stripe of green in moosewood maple,
Color seen in leaf of apple,
   Bark of popple.

Wood of popple pale as moonbeam,
Wood of oak for yoke and barn-beam,
    Wood of hornbeam.

Silver bark of beech, and hollow
Stem of elder, tall and yellow
    Twig of willow.

EDNA ST. VINCENT MILLAY

   The words in the next poem make a kind of music
that you might hear in a children's rhythm band with
lots of triangles and tambourines. Try to memorize
it; it's the kind of thing that's fun to recite in the
shower.

Midsummer Jingle

I've an ingle, shady ingle, near a dusky bosky dingle
Where the sighing zephyrs mingle with the purling of
    the stream.
There I linger in the jungle, and it makes me thrill and
    tingle,
Far from city's strident jangle as I angle, smoke and
    dream.

Through the trees I'll hear a single ringing sound, a
    cowbell's jingle,
And its ting-a-ling'll mingle with the whispers of the
    breeze;
So, although I've not a single sou, no potentate or king'll
Make me jealous while I angle in my ingle 'neath the
    trees.

NEWMAN LEVY

To compose a musical word passage or poem of your own, begin with only two or three words that have similar sounds and are related in meaning. *Slippery, silent snow,* for example, or *rattling skillets and kettles; cawing, squawking crows* or *jostling, rustling bustle.* Now think up other words that have similar sounds and might fit into the meaning of your original group. String them together into a sentence or poem and see how they sound. Make sure they make sense. Here is what a twelve-year-old girl built up from *clicking cricket*:

> The clicking cricket sits on a cracking branch,
> its crackling voice clacking like a clock ticking
> in the crisp darkness.
>
> AMY CASSEDY

Radio and television technicians often use artificial devices to create sounds like those of thunder and howling wind that cannot be naturally reproduced. As a writer, you are your own sound-effects machine, requiring nothing more than pen and paper and a head full of words. You can fill the air with the pinging of sleet against a windowpane or the clang of a brass band marching down the street. There is the sound of singing in the next poem, and of moaning and wailing and groaning. A sound-effects technician might achieve such noises by rattling sheets of metal or blowing across the mouth of an empty bottle. Carl Sandburg used words instead:

Old Deep Sing-song

in the old deep sing-song of the sea
in the old going-on of that sing-song
in that old mama-mama-mama going-on
of that nightlong daylong sleepsong
we look on   we listen
we lay by and hear
too many big bells   too many long gongs
too many weepers over a lost gone gold
too many laughs over light green gold
woven and changing in the wash and the heave
moving on the bottoms   winding in the waters
sending themselves with arms and voices
up in the old mama-mama-mama music
up into the whirl of spokes of light

CARL SANDBURG

19

Rhyme and Rhythm

The very earliest poems were not written down, as they are today, to be read in books and magazines. The poem of long ago was not written down at all; it was sung. Wandering poets known as bards and minstrels would travel from place to place, singing and chanting heroic tales to the accompaniment of small harps. At times someone might dance to the melody of the verse or play along on a pipe. Over the years, as written language developed, poetry became more a thing of the pen than of the voice, but the rhythmic beat and rhyming patterns of the early song remain to this day. The ear delights in a good rhyme and a strong beat, and the voice does too. It is wonderfully satisfying to recite rhyming poetry. It is just as satisfying to make it up.

You have, in fact, quite possibly been making up rhymed poetry since you were very little. All those sing-song teases that you called after your friends in the street—things like "Matt, Matt, your head is fat" or "Ellen, Ellen, watermelon"—are rhymed poems that, like the poems of long ago, are sung and not written. You may even have danced to them.

Such chants are easy to sing or dance to, not only because of their rhymes, but because they possess rhythm, a regular beat that you can clap out or stamp your foot to. All spoken languages contain certain rhythms. In some—French and Japanese, for instance— rhythms are achieved by the rise and fall of the voice or by groupings of syllables. In others, including our own, certain syllables are more heavily accented than others, giving our speech a kind of heavy-light swing. When we say the word *pumpkin*, we put more strength in the first syllable, *pump*, than in the second, *kin*. The first syllable, then, is what we call the accented one, because it has a heavier sound: PUMP-kin. Find the accented syllable in your own name. Like this: CHRIS-to-pher, Me-LISS-a; PE-ter. Now think of a word that has the same beat: CHRIStopher/CHICKen pox; MeLISSa/SpaGHETti; PEter/PURple.

Whole groups of words, when spoken together, also have accented syllables. Find the accents in this sentence: "Mary Jane put bubble gum in Philip Johnson's hair." Recited aloud, the sentence will sound like this: "MARy JANE put BUBble GUM in PHILip JOHN son's HAIR." "DUM dee DUM dee DUM dee DUM dee DUM dee DUM dee DUM." If you clap your hands on each DUM, there will be seven claps all together. Poets call each of these claps—that is, each heavy accent, or DUM—a poetic *foot*. "The BOY upON the JUNgle GYM" has four feet—only in a line of poetry can a boy manage that. Rhythmic poetry is composed of lines like that, whose accented syllables form a steady beat. The pattern of the accents is called the poem's *meter*.

You will notice that in the line about Mary Jane, the meter ran "DUM dee DUM dee DUM dee . . ." while in the line about the boy on the jungle gym, the pattern was reversed: "dee DUM dee DUM dee DUM. . . ." There are several varieties of metrical feet, and each one has a name, derived from the Greek. These are the four most common forms:

IAMB   The word *iamb* (pronounced "EYE-am") possibly comes from a Greek word meaning "lame man." The rhythm of an iamb is "dee-DUM," which suggests the short-LONG step of a limping person. The following poem is written in iambs. Beat out its rhythm with your hand as you read it.

Motto for a Dog House

I love this little house because
   It offers, after dark,
A pause for rest, a rest for paws,
   A place to moor my bark.

ARTHUR GUITERMAN

TROCHEE   A *trochee* (pronounced "TRO-kee") is a metrical foot whose rhythm is "DUM-dee." The word comes from a Greek one meaning "runner," and it may have been used because of the long leap followed by a light step with which a runner sets out on a race. The Three

Witches in William Shakespeare's *Macbeth* recite a stream of LONG-short, LONG-short trochees as they stir their poisonous brew:

> Double, double toil and trouble;
> Fire burn and cauldron bubble.
>
> Fillet of a fenny snake,
> In the cauldron boil and bake;
> Eye of newt and toe of frog,
> Wool of bat and tongue of dog,
>
> Adder's fork and blind-worm's sting,
> Lizard's leg and howlet's wing,
> For a charm of powerful trouble
> Like a hell-broth boil and bubble.

> WILLIAM SHAKESPEARE,
> MACBETH, ACT IV, SCENE I

DACTYL   The rhythm of a *dactyl* (pronounced "DACK-till") sounds like the galloping of a horse: "DUM dee dee." Its name comes from a Greek word meaning "finger," and if you examine one of your own fingers, with its long bone connected to two shorter ones, you will understand why. Listen for the LONG-short-short beat in the nursery rhyme about Moses and his toes:

> Moses supposes his toeses are roses,
> But Moses supposes erroneously.
> Nobody's toeses are posies of roses,
> As Moses supposes his toeses to be.

ANAPEST   An *anapest* (pronounced "AN-a-pest," which comes from a word meaning "reversal," is just the opposite of a dactyl; it is a finger looked at the other way around, "dee-dee-DUM," short-short-LONG. It has a particularly rapid sound and is often used to describe such swift-moving scenes as battlefields and visits from St. Nick. But not always:

from *Portrait of a House*

It is said that mysterious sounds may be heard
In the house when it's empty; but this is absurd.
If you've gone there to listen, it's clear to a dunce
That the house will have ceased to be empty at once.

E. V. RIEU

Poetry can be written with only one or two feet to each line or with as many as five or six or more. When a line has only one foot—and not many poems are written this way—it is called *monometer.* Here is an entire poem written in monometer:

Lines on the Antiquity of Microbes

Adam
Had 'em.

STRICKLAND GILLILAN

Lines with two feet each are more common. They are called *dimeter*, and frequently occur in nursery rhymes and jingles. Here's one:

from *Song of the Pop-bottlers*

Pop bottles pop-bottles
  In pop shops;
The pop-bottles Pop bottles
  Poor Pop drops.

MORRIS BISHOP

It is more common still for a stanza to include lines
with varying numbers of feet. In the following excerpt,
three of the lines have three feet each, which is known as
trimeter; and one line has four feet, which is known as
tetrameter. See if you can identify them.

from *A Bird Came Down the Walk*

A bird came down the walk;
He did not know I saw;
He bit an angleworm in halves
And ate the fellow, raw.

EMILY DICKINSON

In the time of Shakespeare, most poetry was written in
lines of five feet each, or *pentameter*. Count out the five
beats in each of the following lines:

from *Sonnet LXXIII*

That time of year thou mayst in me behold
When yellow leaves, or none, or few, do hang
Upon those boughs which shake against the cold,
Bare ruin'd choirs, where late the sweet birds sang.

WILLIAM SHAKESPEARE

One way to begin writing a rhymed poem of your own is with a name, your own or one you make up. Let's suppose it's Jenny Turner. Listen to its beat, "JENny TURner." Follow it with a phrase that continues that rhythm: "JENny TURner BUMPED her NOSE." Now think of all the words you can that rhyme with *nose: hose, close, rose, suppose.* Don't forget words that are spelled differently but have the same sound, like *grows, toes,* and *froze.* Choose one that you think might fit into the meaning of the first line of your poem. The trouble with writing verses in rhyme is that you often end up saying things that aren't important to the poem in order to work in a rhyme. Sometimes rhyming makes your phrasing unnatural, so your lines may say something like "The hockey stick to him I handed," which is an awkward way to say a simple thing. If a rhyming word forces you to say something you really don't want to say or if it makes your wording clumsy, don't use it. Try another. Or rearrange the words so that the line ends in a different rhyme.

Nose fortunately rhymes with many words, so there is a good chance of finding one that will fit into the meaning of your poem. *Toes* is a possibility. Make up a line ending in "toes" whose beat matches that of "JENny TURner BUMPED her NOSE," and that makes sense in a poem about someone who wasn't watching where she was going—"SCRAPED her KNEES and STUBBED her TOES" might do. You now have a two-line verse. It is called a *couplet.* Verses with three lines are called *triplets*, and four-lined verses are called *quatrains.*

Don't try to cram words against their will into a rhythmic pattern. "Jenny Turner bumped her nose, / fell down over her ice skates and stubbed all of her toes" contains too many beats in the second line, and it is difficult to tell which syllable to stress. Readers don't want to grope about for the beat, nor should they be forced to stress words that would not be stressed in natural speech.

Poetry with a regular, unchanging meter and a steady rhyming pattern sometimes becomes monotonous after a while, and you may want to break up the beat now and then by introducing new rhythms. A poem needn't be written exclusively in trochees or anapests, or any other type of metrical foot. Most poetry today is written with a mixture of them. The following stanza achieves a musical sound through the use of varying rhythmic forms. How many do you find?

from *The Lake Isle of Innisfree*

I will arise and go now, and go to Innisfree,
And a small cabin build there, of clay and
    wattles made;
Nine bean rows will I have there, a hive for
    the honey bee,
And live alone in the bee-loud glade.

WILLIAM BUTLER YEATS

Another way to avoid a singsong quality to your poetry is to allow a sentence to continue from one line to the next, like this:

On a Sundial

I am a sundial, and I make a botch
Of what is done far better by a watch.

HILAIRE BELLOC

For that matter, the rhyming words don't have to occur at the ends of lines at all. They can hide here and there throughout the poem, waiting to surprise. There are several unexpected rhymes and near-rhymes scattered throughout the next poem. See if you can find them.

Greenhouse

In wintertime,
thick flakes sticking to my cheek like licked stamps,
I tramp across the grass
to the greenhouse.

The greenhouse—
that bottle of summer afloat in the snow,
where squads of mottled palm trees grow
and pods like turkey wattles hang—fat, full,
wet with sweat.

The greenhouse!
That's where I go, that's where I stand,
while out in the dark—so cold, so cold—blizzards blow
and scraps of snow die at the walls like froth-winged moths
sizzling in the spark
of a bug trap.

The greenhouse!
That's where I wait, straight and stiff, as if some hand,
some giant hand, might grasp that crooked globe of glass,
and, giving it a sudden shake, let fall another blizzard still:
soft . . . serene . . . a silent storm
of green.

SYLVIA CASSEDY

Poetry can rhyme a little or a lot or not at all, as you see fit. It can follow a rhythm as steady as a drumbeat, or it can skip about here and there wherever you lead it. Usually, when you write poetry, you may be as free as you like. There are, however, certain poetic forms where very strict rules of rhyme and rhythm must be obeyed, and they too are fun to write. The *limerick* is one. Every limerick, in order to deserve the name, must contain five lines that follow a hard-and-fast system of rhythm. Look for it in the following example:

> There was an old man of Peru
> Who dreamed he was eating his shoe.
> He awoke in the night
> In a terrible fright
> And found it was perfectly true.

Clap out the rhythm several times until you have it exactly right. It is essential that the meter of a limerick be perfect. Notice which lines rhyme: one, two, and five have one rhyme sound; three and four have another. As

a beginning, try to compose a limerick from the following opening line:

> There once was a man from Bombay

Another type of poetry with a strict set of rules is the
triolet, a form that originated in France hundreds of years
ago. The triolet is unusual because of the repetition of
some of its lines. Watch for the identical lines in the
following poem. ("Cotoneaster," a flowering shrub, is
pronounced "ka-TOE-nee-ASS-ter.")

Birds at Winter Nightfall

Around the house the flakes fly faster,
And all the berries now are gone
From holly and cotoneaster
Around the house. The flakes fly!—faster
Shutting indoors that crumb out-caster
We used to see upon the lawn
Around the house. The flakes fly faster,
And all the berries now are gone!

THOMAS HARDY

In each triolet the first, fourth, and seventh lines
match one another, although their meanings and punctuation may vary; and the second and eighth lines
match, too. There are only two rhyme sounds, and
they, too, conform to a definite plan. Look back at the
poem above, and follow it: the third and fifth lines
rhyme with the first, and the sixth line rhymes with the

second. It may appear complicated, but in some respects it is easier than other kinds of rhymed poetry. Although it contains eight lines, you have to think up only five of them. Here is an outline for a triolet, containing the two basic lines. Fill in the others, using whatever punctuation suits your meaning.

> Who dangled the bell
> From the neck of the cat
> _____[rhyme with *bell*]
> Who dangled the bell
> _____[rhyme with *bell*]
> _____[rhyme with *cat*]
> Who dangled the bell
> From the neck of the cat

In *terza rima*, which means "third rhyme" in Italian, the rhyme scheme is even more complicated. See if you can figure it out from the next example:

Interlude III

Writing, I crushed an insect with my nail
And thought nothing at all. A bit of wing
Caught my eye then, a gossamer so frail

And exquisite, I saw in it a thing
That scorned the grossness of the thing I wrote.
It hung upon my finger like a sting.

A leg I noticed next, fine as a mote,
"And on this frail eyelash he walked," I said,
"And climbed and walked like any mountain-goat."

And in this mood I sought the little head,
But it was lost; then in my heart a fear
Cried out, "A life—why beautiful, why dead!"

It was a mite that held itself most dear,
So small I could have drowned it with a tear.

KARL SHAPIRO

Each stanza, as you notice, has three lines. The middle line rhymes with the first and third lines of the next stanza, to create a kind of continuous rhyme chain. Here is a beginning stanza for a terza rima you can complete yourself,

Upon the sand there lay a single shell;
All purple-blue it was, like autumn sky;
Within there rose the whisper of a bell

The first and third lines of the next verse will rhyme with "sky." There are five feet in each line; try to retain that form. When you are ready to bring your poem to an end—and there are no set rules for the number of stanzas in *terza rima*—write a couplet that rhymes with the middle line of the preceding verse. Keep checking with the pattern of "Interlude III" whenever you get in trouble.

Poetry with such complicated schemes is often difficult to write, and you may find yourself more involved with the rhymes and meter than with what you want to say, but it can be enormously satisfying to have tackled a poem with a right and a wrong and to know that you've gotten it right.

No matter how rhymes appear in your poetry, whether they march in solemn order or steal in here and there like daisies in a field, they will add the same touch of music and dance that was heard in the song of the minstrel long ago.

20

Poems to Look At

As you have seen, a poem does many things: it sings a song, it screeches and whooshes, it makes you cry or it makes you giggle, and it puts pictures in your head. Now and then a poem does even more—it puts pictures right on the page. Like children of long ago, these poems should be seen and not heard.

A poet's first concern is the words to use. But once you have chosen them for their sound and meaning, you may arrange them on the page, like a handful of colored paper shapes, any way you like, so as to heighten your reader's understanding of what you want to say. Robert Wallace wrote a poem about a snail. These are the words he chose to tell you about it:

This backyard cousin to the octopus sees through two filmy stems on his head, at need can peer round corners, and so betrays his huge timidity. He moves on his single elastic foot seldom, preferring anonymity to danger, seems often to be meditating a very tough problem, likes green leaves and water.

But by placing these same words on the page so that they step along it hesitantly, jerkily, and snaillike, the poet not only tells you about his snail, he shows you as well. Look:

The Garden Snail

This backyard
　　　　cousin
　　　　　　　to the octopus

Sees
　　　　through two filmy
　　　　　　stems

On his head, at
　　　　need
　　　　　　　can peer round

Corners, and
　　　　so betrays his
　　　　　　huge

Timidity. He
　　　　moves on his
　　　　　　single

Elastic foot
　　　　seldom,
　　　　　　　preferring

Anonymity
　　　　to danger,
　　　　　　seems

Often to be
　　　　meditating
　　　　　　a very tough

Problem, likes
        green leaves
            and water.

ROBERT WALLACE

A poet writing about a big, fat thing may put big, fat-sounding words into a big, fat-looking poem, like this:

Plain Talk for a Pachyderm

Spruce up, O Baggy Elephant!
Firm and conform that globular figger,
For, although you yourself may think you've outgrown
    your britches,
Either you've lost weight or your coveralls have stretched:
They appear to be a whole mountain size bigger.

Now, this isn't Skid Row on the Bowery, you know!
You could use a lot more starch in your clothes,
Iron out maybe a billion wrinkles before the next
    opening of the gates,
And tuck up that dangling nose
Which snuffles around your ankles like an old loose
    stocking that got lost from a foot.

You never can tell just who might show up out here, you
    know,
You sloppy pachyderm!
You don't want people whispering amongst themselves,
"Hey, get a load of this big bum!"

PEGGY BENNETT

Or, a poet may make a skinny-looking poem about a skinny-looking thing:

Poem

As the cat
climbed over
the top of

the jamcloset
first the right
forefoot

carefully
then the hind
stepped down

into the pit of
the empty
flowerpot

WILLIAM CARLOS WILLIAMS

Sometimes a poet will arrange the words of a poem so that they become a kind of visual pun. Here the words in a poem about a mirror become the mirror itself:

Mirror

kool uoy nehW	When you look
rorrim a otni	into a mirror
ton si ti	it is not
,ees uoy flesruoy	yourself you see,
dnik a tub	but a kind
rorre hsipa fo	of apish error
lufraef ni desop	posed in fearful
.yrtemmys	symmetry.

JOHN UPDIKE

The next poem leads the reader down the page and then up again, as if on an elevator ride:

Elevator

DOWN	One wall	more.
	a door,	or
	the	away
	others	feet
	bare;	ty
	no	nine-
	win-	later
	dow,	ment
	table,	mo-
	pic-	a
	ture,	just
	chair;	exit
	a gloom-	and
	y,	door
	tomb-	gle
	like	sin-
	room,	its
	and	through
	small—	Enter
	no	vator.
	larger	ele-
	than	the
	a	room
	show-	a
	er	odd
	stall.	How	UP

SYLVIA CASSEDY

In what is known as "concrete poetry," printed words are used like pencil strokes to draw a recognizable shape. Here is an oblong poem that is ready to take off down the sidewalk:

The Sidewalk Racer
or
On the Skateboard

Skimming
an asphalt sea
I swerve, I curve, I
sway; I speed to whirring
sound an inch above the
ground; I'm the sailor
and the sail, I'm the
driver and the wheel
I'm the one and only
single engine
human auto
mobile.

LILLIAN MORRISON

Or words can be pulled apart in bits and pieces, and scattered all over the page in a jumble of letters and punctuation marks that hop about like a grasshopper:

                              r-p-o-p-h-e-s-s-a-g-r
                    who

a)s w(e loo)k
upnowgath
                         PPEGORHRASS
aThe):l   eringint(o-
        eA
            !p:
S   a
                (r
rIvInG   .gRrEaPsPhOs)
                                            to
rea(be)rran(com)gi(e)ngly
,grasshopper;

        E. E. CUMMINGS

   The best subjects for "looking at" poems are those
that have either a shape or a movement that can be easily
drawn. A poem about an airplane can take off from the
bottom corner of a page, rise to the top, perform a loop
or two, and slow down for a landing in the opposite
corner. Or it can nose-dive straight down the middle and
explode at the bottom. A poem about autumn leaves can
scatter its words all over the page or dump them in a
heap along one side. Words can spin on paper like a top,
bounce like a yo-yo, swing like a pendulum, zigzag like
lightning, or crawl like a worm. You can shape them into
zebra stripes, a flight of stairs, a kite, a sailboat, a doughnut, a rainbow, or a dunce cap.

   Remember, though, that all poems must tell something, and while it may be fun to arrange the letters *c-a-t*

all over the page so that they take on the shape of a cat, such a work is not a poem; it is a picture only. It shows, but it doesn't tell. Better to write something out about a cat first, then shape your words into whiskers and a tail.

Index

About the Author

Sylvia Cassedy received her B.A. from Brooklyn College and attended the Johns Hopkins University Writing Seminars. For fourteen years she taught creative writing to children of all ages in libraries, public schools, and private classes.

Her many distinguished books for children include three novels: BEHIND THE ATTIC WALL and M. E. AND MORTON, both of which were ALA Notable Children's Books and *School Library Journal* Best Books of the Year, and LUCIE BABBIDGE'S HOUSE; and a book of poetry, ROOMRIMES.